ENLIGHTENMENT ON THE RUN

ENLIGHTENMENT ON THE RUN

EVERYDAY LIFE AS A SPIRITUAL PATH

Uma Silbey

Airo Press
San Rafael, California

Enlightenment on the Run

First edition
Printed in the United States of America

Cover and text design: Margot Koch, Jim Love
Illustration: Margot Koch
Production consulting: Publisher's Design Studio, Inc.
Production management/composition/page make-up: David Webb

Library of Congress Cataloging-in-Publication Data
Silbey, Uma
Enlightenment on the Run / Uma Silbey.
p.   cm.
ISBN 1-877980-50-1 (pbk.) : $10.95
1. Spiritual life.   2. Spiritual exercises.   3. Conduct of life.
4. Self-realization.   I. Title
BL624S5332 1994
291.4′4—dc20   94-3912
CIP

CONTENTS

V

I *wish to both thank and dedicate this book* to all those friends, family and teachers who have helped me along my path. Most particularly, I wish to dedicate this book to my grandmother, Lloita Glick, who has always inspired me with her quiet dignity and wisdom, to my friend and aunt, Nancy Baumgartner, who has always provided a listening ear and non-judgmental help to me, and who so willingly provides help and comfort to so many. Also to my grandfather, John Reed, who was the first to tell me that I should write books, and to Marcellus Bearheart Williams who has taught me so much in the years I have known him.

I wish to thank my parents, Lloyd Glick and Shirley Murphy, who so unselfishly and lovingly provided me the upbringing in which I could explore myself. Thanks also to: Carol LaRusso and Hal Zina Bennett for all their editing help; to Margot Koch and Jim

Love of Publishers Design Studio for their wonderful book design and illustration; to Brenda Plowman and Dawson Church of Atrium Publishers Group for their thoughtful, expert advice throughout the process; and to David Webb who thought of the title, typeset the book, and has helped in so many other ways to bring it to publication.

Finally, and most importantly, I wish to dedicate this book to my dear husband, Steve Fink, who has always supported and encouraged me through "thick and thin," and to my spiritual guide, teacher and friend, Neem Karoli Baba Ji, who is forever alive within my heart.

May all beings be happy!

Uma Silbey
Lagunitas, California

ENLIGHTENMENT ON THE RUN

INTRODUCTION

*I*t all started when I found a dead bird and lovingly buried him. A couple of days later, curious to see if he had gone to heaven as I'd been told he would, I scraped the dirt from the little grave I had so lovingly made a few days before. As I dug away the rest of the dirt with my little five-year-old hands, slowly the horrible truth revealed itself to me. I was aghast, shocked, for there was the little bird body—still there. Even though I could see that his body was partially decomposed, I didn't think this meant he was halfway to heaven. Instead, I thought that everyone had been lying to me. He wasn't going to heaven—which meant that I wasn't going to

I

heaven, and no one else was either. Who or what
could I believe?

From that point, my search for spiritual truth began. A seed was
planted, and from that seed began sprouting a growing number of
questions and an inner longing for something that I couldn't quite
describe, although it felt like love. I remembered the biblical assur-
ance that all you had to do was knock, and eventually the door would
be opened. You only needed faith and commitment. Being led by
this promise, I vowed to knock until I found the real truth. I didn't
know how I would recognize it, but somehow I knew that I would
know. So through the years I kept knocking.

I started meditating in my late teens. I didn't have any teachers
then, but would acquire books with meditation instructions and do
what they said. At the same time, I continued to live a regular life,
getting a degree at UCLA, starting a jewelry business and doing my
music. To try to understand what the awakening was that I was trying to experience, I proceeded to read every psychological and
philosophical book I could get my hands on, from Dostoyevsky,
Kant, Kierkegaard and Marx to Freud, Jung, Reich, Fritz Perls and
other more modern psychologists. I read, studied and contemplated.
I feasted on ancient scriptures from the Vedas, Puranas, Zen and
other Buddhist texts, the Bhagavad Gita and the Ramayana.

I didn't just read, I practiced what was suggested. I did the rec-
ommended meditations and contemplated Zen koans. I went
through two- and three-year periods of celibacy and retreat. I tried
to understand non-attachment by giving up everything I owned,
household things, businesses, money, and my residence—several

times. Anything that I found myself using to define my identity, I got rid of so I could try and experience my real self. I cut off all my hair (which was quite long), wore white and fasted. I tried to live as consciously and honestly as I could.

I knew that not only did Christians talk about life everlasting, but so did every other scripture that I had ever read. Every one of the scriptures, whether it was Christian, Buddhist, Moslem or Sikh, talked about an eternal state of being that was love itself, undying and unborn, and said there was a path you could travel that would lead you to it. This realization was what was meant by awakening. From my reading, I knew that there were people who had reached this state of enlightenment, and I vowed that if they could do it, so could I. I decided that I would do anything that it took to attain it— whatever *it* was.

For the next twenty-some years I studied with both Eastern and Western teachers. I spent years practicing kundalini yoga, sound and breath meditations, mantra and bhakti yoga, and vipassana meditation, eventually living as a yogi hermit, spending eighteen to twenty hours a day doing these practices. Then I began studying with a Native American Medicine Man based in the Southwest, doing several vision quests and other traditional practices.

It was easy being blissfully peaceful with no distractions, but was it real, or of any use, if it didn't continue when living in the "real" world? So I entered a new phase of my life, diving headlong into everyday living. In the next years (and today), I became a wife and mother, started and grew a sizeable and successful jewelry manufac- turing company with fifteen to twenty employees, managed my home, and continued to write and record ten guided visualization and music recordings. I wrote three books and ran workshops, classes and lectures. Needless to say, I was, (and still am), very busy and carried an incredible amount of responsibility—for my children and family, for my business and employees, and for all the people and projects that I was involved in. I had very little time to do yoga or meditation, and had almost no personal space or time to myself. How could I continue to do the practices I'd been taught? Not only was it impossible to do eight to ten hours of meditation a day, it was impossible to do even five minutes at times!

I looked around and saw others who were in similar positions—career people, professionals, people with their own businesses who raised children and had families, who struggled with a similar dilemma: How could we keep up our lifestyle with busy schedules, very little or no personal space, endless responsibilities, and still remain on a spiritual path that would bring inner peace and love into our lives? How could we stay centered, have a calm mind, stay healthy and keep from losing our way in the everyday hustle and bustle of life? As a friend of mine expressed, "I feel like I have to make a choice, either chucking it all and going to live in an ashram, or staying in my impossibly busy life where I'm sacrificing my peace of mind!"

Out of necessity I started adapting the practices I had been taught to the realities of my busy life. I began asking some new questions about them: What practices had the maximum effect in the shortest time? What could be done "on the run?" What could be done so that I could maintain my spiritual center, my inner peace, and stay relaxed and full of energy? What kept me constantly in touch with the inner, guiding Spirit in spite of a daily onslaught of household demands, difficult business obligations, broken appointments, constantly ringing phones, impossible schedules and almost no "time for myself?" What was the essence contained in all of the various traditions and practices that I'd worked with, and how could it be organized, practiced and realized in a very busy life such as the one that I was leading? How could life, itself, become my practice?

This book is the result of my efforts to bring these practices into everyday life. In it I describe six practices that you can do during your normal life that will lead you to a state of awareness, wisdom, inner peace and Self-discovery—practices that really work in a busy, modern life, and not just in the rarefied atmosphere of the ashram or retreat facility. These six practices can be applied to all the real things that you have to deal with in life: being too busy, having families, working, responsibility, relationship, loss, doubt, fear, anger, pride, sickness, birth, death and love. The practices are practical techniques, helping you find your way when you feel overwhelmed, confused or lost. This book is not only meant to instruct, but also to be a companion on your personal journey. Ultimately, what I have written here is a sharing of my heart, so that together we can celebrate the endless presence of living Spirit. Through this sharing, may we inspire each other and come to fully appreciate the infinite reality within that will guide us to know the truth contained in our own souls.

DANCE EVER SO LIGHTLY

Do you love what can never
    be understood by the mind?
Do you hear the truth
    which speaks beyond words?

Then you are one of those blessed
    to carry love's flame in your soul,
    to plant seeds of charity,
    and reflect the Great Light within.

So sharpen your discrimination
    upon the millstone of experience,
    and with integrity unconquered
    embrace its crystalline wisdom.

Then dance ever so lightly
    with dawn's light in you eye,
    sweet laughter in your heart,
    and fire in your soul.

Oh, fortunate one,
    cry out your fulfillment
    with tears of diamond love,
    for you are eternally blessed and free.

Be Who You Really Are
And Walk The Path
To Your Own Awakening.

CHAPTER ONE

The Six Practices

*M*ost spiritual traditions instruct you to
take some amount of time away from
everyday living in order to look inward, insisting
that this is the only way to become enlightened
and find true happiness. This may range from
an hour or two a day, to years in solitary retreat—or even leaving the everyday world alto-
gether. Perhaps the most recent variation of this
philosophy was succinctly expressed by Timothy
Leary in the 60's as "Turn on, tune in and drop
out." This is not always practical or desirable,
however, when you have children, have to earn a
living or have other responsibilities.

In this book you'll discover that you don't have to drop out or do drugs to "tune in" or "turn on." Nor do you have to ignore the external world in order to look inward. Instead, you'll use each thing in life as a stepping stone on your own spiritual path. Through the exercises and practices presented here you will use life itself to become aware of a living reality that exists within and without, always there in spite of the constant ebb and flow of emotions, thoughts and life events. You'll be able to live your outward life in harmony with this inner reality, bringing yourself deep fulfillment, internal freedom and inward contentment. You'll be able to be happy—no matter what your life is like.

Normal Versus Spiritual Life

There are many teachings, both ancient and modern, that talk about enlightenment, about knowing who we are or experiencing a reality beyond the one we ourselves project to the world. There are also hundreds of ancient, well-tested methods to help us see past what is called the world's "illusion" in order to experience a deeper happiness that doesn't depend on the circumstances of our life. But most of the time the practices associated with traditional spiritual teachings require us to retreat from daily life. They often instruct different forms of abstinence, celibacy, silent retreat, fasting or eating only certain foods. Long hours of meditation, prayer or yoga are required for many years in a traditional spiritual lifestyle.

These practices do help us acquire peace of mind, concentration and quietness; we can even become wise and enlightened through them. But in modern life this inner quietness and sense of enlightenment begins to disappear as soon as we come back to everyday life. Somehow, we can't quite seem to carry the effects of our practices and realizations into contemporary living.

In light of this, we have to wonder if these types of spiritual paths have any relevance to the ordinary person. The practices seem impossible to do if we also have to answer telephones, pick kids up from school, earn a living, cook meals for our family or keep up with all the constant responsibilities that we have in our life. These practices don't seem to offer any practical help with everyday living as so often their effects keep disappearing as soon as we get back to our everyday life.

As a result, many of us have given up and assumed that we can never find the inner freedom that we're looking for because we're living an everyday life. After all, we can't leave our family, job or other responsibilities. Many of us may feel stuck and somewhat resentful of our everyday lifestyle that seems to have robbed our lives of adventure, purpose and even love. Somewhere, deeply within us we may feel a vague longing or an ache for something that we can't even articulate. It seems as if life has us trapped.

I remember feeling this way when I moved up to San Francisco in 1981 from Los Angeles. For years my life in Los Angeles had been based around various spiritual practices, culminating in two years or so in celibate retreat, spending up to twenty hours or so a day doing kundalini yoga and various other forms of meditation. Now, living in San Francisco, I was involved in a lifestyle that was completely different! I was beginning a crystal jewelry business, writing books, recording, teaching, managing an organization, getting married and raising a family. I was so busy trying to meet my responsibilities that keeping up with my old spiritual life became impossible. I felt a vague sense of loss and guilt. I felt increasingly frustrated the busier I became and the less free time I had just to relax and be inward. Should I do less? Should I drop out again? In struggling with this dilemma, I finally realized that the only way that it would work was to make my everyday life my practice. So out of all the practices I had done in the past, I began to do those that were most practical, that could be done inconspicuously anywhere, anytime. Because I had so little free time I did the practices that were effective most quickly. As a result, my normal life became my entire path. I found that the spiritual and material life don't have to be opposed to each other. You don't have to leave the world in order to live a life of Spirit. You can live a spiritual life whether you're a householder or a monk, a mother or a nun, a business person or a yogi.

Your Daily Life is Fuel for Your Path

*T*he practices that are presented here are perfectly suited for a busy, modern lifestyle. Rather than being a hindrance, your daily routine can literally become the focal point for spiritual practice. You don't necessarily do any more or less than normal when you are doing these practices, nor is your routine intrinsically bad or good for them. The focus of your life is more important than the form in which you live it. What is most important is your intention, how you regard and work with your life events. Instead of ignoring feelings, thoughts and other things happening to you, you use these practices to dive into them. There is no avoidance of any part of yourself, only complete acceptance.

The Practices

The six interrelated practices that make up this path are deceptively simple, yet as you do them you'll find that they eventually lead to great depths of understanding and wisdom. These six practices, which are individually explained in the following six chapters, are:

1. Be Present-Centered

2. Observe

3. Remember

4. Follow Truth

5. Accept

6. Meditate

The practices are like the threads that form the woof and warp of a single woven tapestry. To experience the strand is to experience its interweaving, which is to ultimately experience the entire tapestry. Each practice supports each one of the others. As you practice one, you practice the others. You will find, for example, that when you are present-centered, you are also in a state of observation. When you observe you experience the truth. Observing the truth is to remember, which is also a meditation. When you are in a state of meditation, you are present-centered. Each of these practices also stands as a single pathway; each one capable of completely guiding you to awareness.

Here is another way to view these practices:

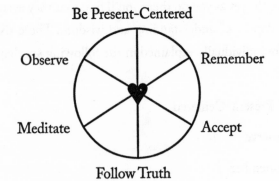

Be Present-Centered

Observe

Remember

Meditate

Accept

Follow Truth

In The Center
They Are One

Finding The Time

You don't need lengthy time periods to do these practices. Start by taking three minutes a day to breathe with long deep breaths while you forget everything else, even if you're at your office desk or standing in line at the bank. Find a few moments to stretch your body, meditate, contemplate or exercise. Be creative. Find where you can make some personal space in your life if you don't have it now. If you're working, take lunch or a fifteen minute break by yourself. Turn off the TV for a half hour (or more) at night. Put your book down. Get up even fifteen minutes earlier in the morning. Take an early morning walk or do them while you're driving to work. If you're shopping, instead of racing down the aisles, walk slowly and take your time. If you're putting your children to sleep, spend a few silent moments with your eyes closed also. Take a warm, soothing bath instead of your usual quick shower. Take a few extra moments enjoying the morning as you go outside to get the newspaper. Be creative. Don't deny yourself this time. With a minimum of commitment this can be done even in the busiest of lives. With commitment, you will find more and more times in your life where you can assign this personal quiet space to yourself.

Before long you will find that these practices become a natural part of your day. Eventually, your inward focus will become inseparable from your outward focus, much like in-breath following outbreath. The distinction between time for yourself and time that's not for yourself will disappear. All time will become time for yourself, because everything that you will be doing will be also be developing your own self-awareness. Your entire life will serve to nurture you instead of deplete you. This doesn't mean that you won't ever get tired, or won't need time to relax your body or mind. It just means that you will be able to find fulfillment, even when you are impossibly busy, tired or relaxed.

Follow these six practices and let your daily routine become a grand adventure instead of something just to be endured. Fill your life with exciting discovery and meaning, even in the midst of difficulty. Best of all, do these practices and eventually you will find deep fulfillment as you experience the heart of your inner self, the joyful beingness that also lies at the center of all creation. This kind of awakening will bring you happiness beyond even the most exciting rewards of the modern world.

THE WAY

Come forward, my friend,
*   don't be faint hearted.*
Don't let this Way's wild turbulence
*   lessen your will to be free.*

Hold fast to the sight
*   of your hopes and dreams,*
*   as you fearlessly travel the lands*
*   that call to your aching heart.*

Be unafraid as you cross
*   empty deserts of confusion.*
*   and wander through*
*   midnight valleys of fear.*

Fly, my friend.
Trust the wings of love
*   that transport you through*
*   these vast distances of not-knowing.*

Trust and be carried
*   faithfully to the home*
*   that has been calling so sweetly*
*   in the night whispers of your soul.*

CHAPTER TWO

Be Present-Centered

The First Practice

*T*he first of the six practices is to be present-
centered. This is one of the most important
practices because you can't master any of the
others without mastering this one. The more that
you're centered in the present, the more depth
you'll achieve when you do the other practices.
What does it mean to be present-centered? To be
present-centered means very simply to be here
now. To be here now is to have your entire awareness centered right here where you are instead of
thinking about yesterday or tomorrow. You're not
even thinking of the last second. You're aware of

your feelings now, rather than comparing them to
past feelings or how you might be feeling in the
future. Neither are you thinking that you should
or could be feeling differently than you are now.
To be present is to let go of every other awareness
and experience yourself totally as you really are in
each moment.

How does this translate into daily living? Simply this: If you're present-centered as you drive your car, you're aware of the motions of your body as you drive, the sounds that you're hearing, the feeling of the car seat beneath you and the sensation of speed. You aren't thinking of your workday, the coming weekend, what you should have done or will be doing next. If you are cooking a meal, you're aware of the motions of your spoon in the bowl, the smell of the ingredients, the heat of the oven, the sounds of the boiling water and the cutting of your knife. You are completely focused on cooking. If you are present-centered in this way, every action becomes a meditation in complete awareness. Not only this, but practically speaking, living becomes much more interesting as your range of experience widens. Even the most mundane things in your life become very interesting as you notice things that you never noticed before, even if they're things that you don't usually enjoy. Walking out to your car in the morning, for example, becomes so much richer an experience when you take the time to notice the earth that you are walking on, the air that you're breathing and your feelings at the time.

What is it like to be present-centered? When you are completely here in the present, there is a sense of time slowing or stopping. Each moment becomes an eternity beyond time. If you stop comparing one moment to another, how can you have a sense of time's passage? Do you remember how long a day was when you were a child with no concerns other than what you were doing? Do you remember how free you felt? This is what it feels like to be centered in the present. When you are here now, there is a feeling of being collected within yourself instead of feeling frantically scattered outward. You feel as if you have a center to you which gives you a feeling of inner security. Instead of a galloping mind, your thoughts seem to slow down so that you become aware of each single thought—and eventually the spaces between thoughts. Instead of racing emotions, your feelings become calm. You feel as if you are a deep, still pool of water inside.

The more you become focused in the present moment, the more this calmness will increase. How can you worry or be afraid if you are not thinking of the future, for example? How can you feel guilty or resentful if you are not thinking of the past?

Know Who You Are

*I*t is only when you are centered in this present moment that you can begin to know who you really are. The "you" that can be known is only here, nowhere else, so if you aren't here, centered in the present, where is the "you" to experience? If your thoughts and feelings are racing outwards in all directions, how can you possibly focus inward? You can't. If you allow your mind to endlessly chase after every passing thought and emotion, all you are aware of are the thoughts and emotions, not yourself. Being present means shifting your attention back to yourself. It means focusing on the "you" that is experiencing these thoughts and emotions. Then you become *you, the experiencer.* When you are aware of yourself as the experiencer, you will notice that you are separate from whatever is experienced. You are being you, and you are merely having thoughts and feelings. You are being, not having. So when you focus on you, the experiencer, you shift your focus to your own beingness.

Now do this: Shut your eyes for a moment and focus on yourself. Feel yourself as "you." Don't try to explain or define yourself. Just get a sense of the "you" that is inside your body. If you become distracted by thoughts or feelings, just drop your attention from them and bring it back to your sense of being "you." Where are you? Can you define the space that you occupy? Can you find any edges to yourself? Do you have a sense of being in your body? Are you outside of your body? Keep focusing on your sense of "you" at the same time that you ask yourself these questions: Where are you? Can you come up with any other answer other than you are *here*? Now remember yourself in a past situation. Recreate that situation in your mind and put yourself there. Now, while you are still reliving that situation as if you are there now, ask yourself the same question. Where are you? Not, where is your body or where is your mind, but where is the "you" that is having thoughts and feelings and causing your body to move? All you can say is that you are *here*. Similarly, think about your dreams. At the time that you're dreaming, aren't you usually only aware of yourself as being "here" in your dream? Aren't you still the one experiencing and acting?

Have you ever been aware of a time that you were not here, whether in the past, present or in your dreams? No. You are always *here*. This is true in spite of the fact that your thoughts and feelings always change. You're always here, even though your body has completely changed over the years. You have a sense of being "here" even when you are in the dream state, and even when you are in an altered state of consciousness. So even though everything about you changes, you are always *here*.

In order, then, to know who you really are, you need to constantly bring your focus back to here. Where is here? It is the present moment. To live consciously, in complete self-awareness is to let go of each past moment and open to what is here now. As you slow down and center into the present, each moment will expand to include worlds of meaning and new experience. It's as if time stands still and you enter a whole new universe. It is here that inspiration, intuition and creativity are born. It's here that you relax and gain true inner refreshment and renewal. Your entire being expands past any limitation. Instead of just enduring the onslaught of daily pressures, you'll be able to relax and dive into them, moment to moment. When you do that, even the most difficult experiences become your food for growth and personal expansion.

Three Steps to Being Present-Centered

What do you do to be present-centered? The instructions are easy:

1. Anytime that you discover that you are *thinking* of anything else other than what you are doing in the present moment, let those thoughts go and bring all of your attention back to *now*.

2. As soon as you are aware that your *feelings* are taking you away from your present focus, drop your attention from them and bring it back to what you are doing *now*.

3. Keep your awareness totally focused here, now, no matter what you are doing.

The breathing exercise at the end of this chapter will help you develop the ability to become present-centered. The eating meditation will show you how even a mundane activity can be used for awakening. Let these exercises teach you, and then apply what you've learned to the rest of your life.

The key is to *use every event and action in your life as an opportunity to be entirely here now.* The largest practical problem faced in living a "householder" lifestyle instead of in the simplified environment of the ashram or retreat space is how to handle your responsibilities, remember everything and get things done without having so much on your mind that you are no longer focused on the here and now. You don't have this problem in the ashram or retreat space—from personal experience. Now I run a good-sized business, have a family, manage a household, write books and record music and sponsor meditation events. In a busy life such as this, there is a way to empty your mind of the future so that you can bring it to the present.

The solution is to *write things down.* Don't try to store so much in your mind. Get a good calendar to record what you have to do as it comes up. *Once you do this, stop thinking about it.* Drop all thoughts of what you have to do from your mind and return to the present. Perhaps do a few long deep breaths to help you.

Write down things that you want to remember, whether it's short-term or long-term. Keep a separate book of thoughts and ideas so you don't have to worry about forgetting them. Keep all calendars and notes where they are handy at all times.

Be Aware of Your Thoughts

With practice it will become easier for you to become present-centered. Eventually it will become automatic. At first, however, being present-centered requires constant vigilance. For example, how many times have you driven someplace only to find that you can't even recall the drive? Where were you when your body was automatically driving the car? How many times have you not heard someone speaking to you when you were thinking of something else? You will find yourself drifting away from the here and now like this over and over again during the day.

When you find that you have drifted this way, or your thoughts have wandered into the future or past, just let them go and bring your focus back to the present. To do this, you can use the following technique:

1. Take a long deep breath, feeling as if you are being pulled back into yourself as your breath enters.

2. As your breath leaves, allow yourself to relax. Let go of your clenched stomach, and the tension in your jaw, the small of your back and the backs of your knees. Let your shoulders drop and feel your feet as being solidly on the earth.

3. As you relax and breathe, bring yourself back to here.

When you are thinking, be aware that you are thinking instead of letting your mind wander, carrying you away with it. Be entirely focused on each thought. If you are figuring out what movie to see, for example, don't at the same time plan what time to get the babysitter, what you're going to feed the kids, how tired you'll be in the morning, whether you'll be able to do your work the next day, etc. You don't have to take a lot of time to focus on each thought. This can be done with lightning speed if necessary.

Think of one thing at a time and make one decision at a time. When you are thinking of many things at once rather than one at a time, you are never entirely focused on any one thought. Instead, you're focused on nothing—and then you are nowhere.

When you are only partially focused on your thoughts, feelings or actions, this not only carries you away from your present awareness but it never allows you to entirely drop them from your conscious or subconscious attention. They begin to pile up in your mind. This is what produces feelings of being scattered, anxious or overwhelmed. As your mind starts racing from half-thought to thought, your feelings likewise will become jumbled and confused. When you experience this too long, you eventually either "fall apart," or handle it by feeling partially or totally empty inside, divorced from your inner self. It is only by becoming more present-centered that you reverse this process and can begin to find your way through life's maze of problems, pressures and frustrations.

In order to be present-centered, you don't have to stop having feelings or thoughts. Just don't lose yourself in them. If you are thinking, be entirely focused on each thought as it comes up. Then let it go completely as it leaves you. If you are feeling angry, don't feel only part of your anger, or your anger and everything else at the same time. Just feel your anger now, moment to moment as it is happening.

Being present-centered doesn't necessarily mean that you'll now only have "good" feelings instead of "bad" feelings. However, you will find that as you become more present-centered, you won't get as angry, depressed, anxious, or overwhelmed. As this happens, the content of your feelings often change for the better.

The following are two exercises that you can do to become more present-centered. You can do them nearly anytime during your day: while watching your kid at the park, cooking a meal, doing your work, or watching TV. You can also do these as a regular meditation, setting aside an hour, half hour, or even a few minutes every day.

Long Deep Breathing
Meditation to Become
Present-Centered

This is one of the most simple yet effective meditations that you can do. The effects are many. You will become present-centered. Your mind and emotions will be calm and your body will relax. You'll feel expanded and filled with a sense of well being as your heart opens to the love that is always within you. When your heart center is open, you will be able to express yourself emotionally, feel compassion and empathy. This meditation will help bring you into a state of natural balance and develop the ability to effortlessly concentrate your mind to think clearly. This is an excellent meditation to do regularly once a day for three minutes, ten minutes or any time up to an hour. Though you may feel a difference the first time you practice, most of the effects are cumulative and will develop over time.

The Meditation

1. Sit comfortably with your spine straight, your feet on the ground, legs uncrossed, your chin level and your eyes closed.

2. If appropriate, bring your palms together as if you are praying and rest the sides of your hands against the middle of your chest with a slight pressure. You can also rest your hands in your lap.

3. Breathe slowly and deeply in through your nose, completely filling your lungs without straining or gasping. Feel the breath enter your nose and move down to fill your lungs.

4. When your lungs are filled, slowly exhale through your nose, feeling as if all tension leaves with your breath. Relax and completely empty your lungs without gasping or straining.

5. As you breathe, completely focus all of your attention on the breath as it flows in and out of your body. If thoughts or emotions arise, just notice them and let them go. Continually bring your attention back to your breath. No matter what else you may see, hear or feel, notice it and bring your attention back to your breath. Eventually the workings of your mind and emotions will become still and your attention will become effortlessly focused. You will go deeper and deeper into yourself.

6. With time, your breath will become increasingly slower, with distinct spaces between the in-breath and the out-breath. At this time, focus both on the breath and the spaces between the breath. At no time should you strain, gasp or try to forcefully slow your breath.

7. You will feel more and more deeply relaxed. At times, you may feel as if you are so light that you are floating. Don't let this sensation distract your attention. Just

notice, and bring your attention back to your
breathing.

8. Repeat this long deep breathing until you feel calm
   and centered or for at least three minutes to start.
   Increase the time as you feel ready. You will know
   when you are centered because you will feel as if you
   are filled with a deep peacefulness. You will feel as if
   you are gathered into your center with no intruding
   thoughts and emotions. With practice, you will feel as
   if you are just beingness, beyond body and thought.
   You will feel complete and whole in yourself, and
   totally fulfilled.

Eating Meditation To Become Present-Centered

The following is a meditation that you can do while eating to learn
to become present-centered. As a side benefit, you will eat more
slowly, chew more completely, taste more and digest your food better. You will become more aware of your body's internal signals so
that you start being more conscious of what you eat, how much you
eat and its effect on you. When you pay attention to your eating this
way, you'll notice what foods make you feel better or worse, and will
naturally, then, start eating what's healthier for you. You'll also eat

less. This is also a good meditation, then, to lose weight and improve
your health through conscious eating. You can do this eating meditation alone or with your entire family.

The Meditation

1. Close your eyes for a couple of moments, collecting
    yourself with your in-breath and relaxing with your
    out-breath. Do this for three or four breaths. If you
    like, further "tune in" by taking a few moments to feel
    thankfulness for your life, for your food and for the
    plants and animals that have given their lives that you
    may live.

2. Open your eyes and gaze at the food on your plate.
    Notice what it looks like. Notice its colors, odors,
    arrangement and other attributes.

3. Now begin to eat. As you do, be aware of the action of
    picking up your eating utensil. Notice how your hand
    grasps the utensil. Be aware of the cutting, scooping,
    stabbing, scraping and other actions as you pick up the
    food to bring it to your mouth. Be aware of your arm
    bending and any other body action as you bring the
    food to your mouth.

4. Next, notice how you bite the food. Feel your teeth
    touching and your jaw moving as you begin to bite
    into the food. Notice the heat or coldness, the texture
    and the softness or hardness of the food as you bite
    into it.

5. Now, as you chew your food, feel your teeth touching
    and your jaw continuing to move. Feel your tongue as
    it moves the food around in your mouth. Notice where
    the food touches your tongue and the inside of your
    mouth. How does it feel in your mouth? Notice the
    saliva as it enters and joins with the food and the
    changing texture and temperature of the food as it is
    chewed.

6. After experiencing the chewing of the food, swallow
    and be aware of it as it passes down your throat,
    esophagus and into your stomach. Can you feel the
    warmth or coldness as it passes? Notice how your
    stomach feel as it fills with food. Notice any other
    sensations that you feel in your body as it fills with
    food.

7. As you bite, chew and swallow, notice the taste of the
    food without evaluating how good or bad it is. Just

notice how it tastes. Notice any after-taste that lingers in your mouth after you have swallowed.

8.   As you do this, let all thoughts, evaluations, feelings and other distractions go. Just notice them, and then let them go from your mind, focusing again on the food and your eating process.

9.   Notice your eating pace. Are you concentrating on getting more food to put in your mouth before you have even tasted what you have in there now? If so, you're cheating yourself of completely tasting and otherwise experiencing your food. Take a moment to feel your body. Notice if you have had enough to eat, if you feel full. If you are, stop eating.

10.   When you are done eating, focus on the action of putting your eating utensils down and taking your napkin off of your lap (if you are using one).

11.   Notice how you feel after finishing your meal. Notice if you feel satisfied. Do you taste any aftertaste of the food? Do you feel the warmth of a full stomach? Take a few moments to be aware of any emotions or

thoughts that you have that are associated with the meal. After noticing them, let them go. Be aware of what you do to signal the end of your meal. Now with complete awareness, arise from the table.

As you learn to be more in the here and now by doing this eating meditation, you will notice many other areas in your life where you can apply the same technique. For example, you can focus in the same way that you do in this meditation while brushing your teeth, taking a shower, dressing, walking, changing diapers or driving a car. The main thing when using daily life events as your meditation, is to focus as completely as possible on every action, perception and sensation so that you are completely here now. When you are perceiving and acting from a position of being present-centered, even these more mundane life events will offer you realization.

BEING HERE

When you are here
   It doesn't have anything to do
   With what's around you.

Because—

Being Here
   Is beyond such considerations
   As time, space and matter.

To be here
   Is to be everywhere and nowhere
   At the same time.

In fact—

There is nowhere else
   You ever are
   But here.

When you are here
   Your life is
   Endless.

*ULTIMATELY
LOVE IS THE CENTER
OF ALL CREATION*

CHAPTER THREE

Observe

The Second Practice

*T*o observe is to notice your experience,
    moment by moment in the "here and now"
without the interference of your judgments,
hopes, opinions, definitions, doubts, fears or
other mental/emotional reactions. When you
observe, you just take note, without taking action
or making a decision about what you notice. It is
important to be as honest as you can possibly be
with yourself so that you can experience the way
something actually is rather than how you would
like it to be or how you might fear it to be.

There is nothing in life that you can't observe, whether it be thoughts, feelings, appearances, motivations, cause and effect relationships or anything else. You can notice everything in the world around you.

When you can observe things as they are, rather than how you think or believe them to be, your understanding will grow and you will gain real wisdom. Observation has many practical benefits as well. With observation, for example, you'll find that your actions and decisions will become more effective and appropriate to the real situation, whether it be at home or at work. When you can observe and relate to yourself as you really are, you can do the same with others. You'll begin to have relationships that are deeper and more fulfilling than ever before.

Seeing and the Process of Separation From Self

It can be helpful to think in terms of there being two distinctively different processes—"seeing" and "observing." Think of seeing as separating yourself from what you're looking at in order to name, compare, contrast, react or make other decisions or assumptions in order to describe it to yourself. (This is true not only when you see, but also when you receive information through any of your five senses.) It's as if there is a voice in your head that keeps up a running commentary on what you are viewing or sensing, constantly interpreting your experiences instead of simply letting you take them in. A friend of mine once compared this interpretive voice to the experience of going to a movie with someone who talks through the whole thing, telling you what's coming next or giving his or her opinions about every scene! The effect of this kind of "seeing" is to distance you from the world, creating a sense of separation that can be quite uncomfortable, robbing you of enjoying the real richness and beauty of your life.

You learn this process of separation as you grow from a newborn and learn to differentiate what you see into separate objects. It's part of the naming process that we learn from our parents and the entire culture around us: "Look at the ducky." "Here is mommy." "Here is your bottle." This process intensifies as you develop language. Finally you do this continually with everything that you see, faster than conscious thought. Like breathing, it's done so automatically that you aren't aware of the process unless you consciously focus on it.

This process of separation and objectifying isn't wrong. You need to do this in order to speak, to relate to others and otherwise function in daily life. However, every time that your mind assigns a name to what you see, you limit your experience, forcing it to fit into your own mental description. Your world shrinks into a "manageable" size. You stop directly experiencing your world first hand, and instead experience it according to how it conforms to a set of pictures, words and interpretations you are storing in your mind. When you look at a tree, for example, you automatically "know" that it is green and brown, and the leaves move because of the wind. You "know" even without looking, that it grows out of the dirt, so it requires only a cursory glance to confirm the fact that the brown earth is there. You might take another glance to notice that there is also green at the base of the tree, which you know is grass. Because you "know" what trees, dirt and grass look like, (based on shared characteristics of past similar objects), you don't feel that you need to look further to see them. Following this example, you probably wouldn't even notice the white birds hidden in the branches, the fruit scattered on the ground beneath it, or the girl peeking from behind the trunk. Because you didn't bother to look more closely, you only saw what you "knew" instead of what was really there. How much of the physical world around us we miss because of this!

We also limit our experience of ourselves and others when we judge or objectify, such as: "I'm fat!" "You're beautiful!" "I'm confused!" Or: "We're good, they're bad;" "We're happy, they're unhappy;" "I'm Julie..." "I'm Ted..." "I know...I don't know!" "They're students." "I'm a father." Endlessly, we automatically categorize and name ourselves and others, growing increasingly separate from our direct inner experience of self and others. We forget that everything in the world, including each other, is constantly changing and cease to see what is fresh and new as each moment unfolds. Over and over we relate to what we "know" about another rather than more deeply experiencing them as they really are. How easy it is for relationships to become shallow, boring and trite when we unwittingly objectify and encapsulate each other.

How limiting our relationships can be as we unwittingly hold each other apart through our judgments and interpretations.

Observation

With observation this process of separation is reversed and you can begin to experience yourself and your life more directly. When you observe, you don't hold yourself apart from that which you see, because you don't try to label or describe it. To observe is to see past the surface characteristics of things, to momentarily let go of all your "knowing" to see what is really so. To observe is to let go of what you "know" in order to experience yourself and the world as fresh and new, a moment that has never existed before and will never exist again.

Think how interesting it is to experience something new! When something is new, it totally captures our attention. Imagine this: Someone says to you that they're going to give you a bite of the best-tasting dessert that they had ever had in their entire life. "This is so good that it's going to blow your mind!" they say to you. Now imagine that they begin to bring a spoon to your lips with a big bite of it. You look at the bite on the spoon, open your mouth, and with total concentration you begin tasting the flavor of the most scrumptious dessert that you can imagine. Filling your mouth, for a few moments you're aware only of the exquisite taste as, swallowing, you enjoy the sensation of the flavor lingering in your mouth.

Now contrast this with our normal style of eating. It's much less fun! We don't usually enjoy each bite to the degree that we did the new dessert. In fact, most of the time we're busy talking and doing other things so much when we eat that we barely taste our food. Our attention is focused elsewhere. It's easy to eat an entire meal and not even remember much about it, other than to somewhat automatically categorize it as "good," "not good," "hot," "too dry," "just how you like it," etc. Think about how much more interesting the bite was of the brand new dessert that you tasted. Then you were totally involved, not thinking about anything else, relaxed, and totally yourself in the moment. This is like observation. When you observe, life gets much more interesting, just as that bite of dessert was. You feel more involved, present, expanded and alive.

In the act of observing, you're so involved that you don't "know" anything. In tasting the dessert, you didn't know what it would taste like. You just tasted it. Like the moment of first tasting the dessert, your mind empties, no longer figuring, inferring, deducing, categorizing or naming. To observe, then, is the opposite of ordinary seeing. There is no sense of "you" as distinct and separate from the "other." That part of you which constantly analyzes, compares, contrasts and otherwise maintains your independent identity, is silent. Instead, you have a sense of merging with or being in complete harmony with the world. When you observe, you feel, you intuit and ultimately get in touch with your deeper inner knowing. The more that you practice observation, the more this inner sense of knowing opens to you.

Observation can only be done in the present, not in the past or the future. You can only observe what is actually here now. The past is like a shadow, only a memory stored in your mind. You can't observe the actual past. You can, however, observe yourself recalling the past and the pictures of the past that you hold in your mind. Similarly, you cannot observe the future, that is, what is yet to happen. You can only observe the pictures in your mind or yourself in the action of fearing, imagining, hoping, or inferring what might be. The more that you can be centered in the here and how, rather than in the future or past, the more will be available for your observation.

You'll be amazed at what will begin to happen the more that you observe. The veils of objectifying and naming, which previously hid the world from you, and you from yourself, will slowly be removed. Your world will expand beyond what you've imagined as you begin to experience what you'd been blind to before. The world will come out of hiding, revealing its true nature. Your inner self will come out of hiding also. You'll be able to learn so much more about the people and life around you as your vision widens. Your relationships with people will deepen as you're able to relax, be more vulnerable and relate to others as they are inside. You'll become more intuitive, inspired, energetic and creative. For most of us, this doesn't happen overnight. But by just being willing to slow down and "know" a little less, and taking the time to look, it does begin to happen more and more. So be patient with yourself. Stick to the observation practice and it will most assuredly come.

Meditation:
How To Observe

The following are the instructions for observation. The first few times you do it, be in a place free of distractions and free of the possibility of being interrupted. Start with just a few minutes of practice and eventually, if you like, increase your time up to an hour a day. By doing this you will learn to observe. Then, incorporate this practice into your daily life. You can observe anything at anytime, be it at work, at home, in the car, being with friends or strangers.

If you don't have the time to start this practice as a longer exercise first done in isolation at home, go ahead and immediately incorporate it into your daily life. Many people start observing while they are doing routine tasks such as jogging, walking, washing the dishes or running copies at work.

The Meditation

1. Choose an object, a feeling, thought or action that you want to observe. Begin to focus all of your attention on it. For example, if doing this exercise in private, you might light a candle and observe it. Or you might observe a flower or a feeling of sadness or joy you happen to experiencing at the time.

2. Continue to notice more and more about the action,
    object, feeling or thought. As you focus your attention
    in this way, you may notice how thoughts and feelings,
    or your inner "interpretive" voice starts intruding. At
    this point it's not important to know that you do not
    have to allow your attention to shift to these
    "intruders." Let the intruder enter, acknowledge its
    presence, then let it go, shifting your attention back to
    your chosen focus. (For example, while doing this
    exercise recently, I kept having a troubling thought
    about my business intrude. I finally had to say to
    myself, "Okay, I have noted the problem and I will
    take care of it later. But for now I choose to focus my
    attention on my meditation.") Continue emptying
    your mind this way, continually bringing your
    attention back to what you are observing.

3. If you feel yourself getting tense, focus for a moment
    on the area of tension. Then, let those muscles gradu-
    ally relax, becoming softer, warmer, more comfortable.
    If you like, use your breath to relax. Let out the
    tension with your out-breath and feel yourself bring-
    ing in peacefulness with your in-breath. Continue to
    observe as you do this.

4. Be gentle with yourself. Do not force yourself to
    concentrate or try to not think. If you do this, your
    mind and emotions will race even more.

Don't be afraid to notice everything that you can. Be impecca-
bly honest with yourself. This will help you develop your skill. The
more skilled you are in your observation, the more underlying
subtleties you will see. You'll discover hidden motivations and underlying emotions. You'll be able to notice the continual interplay
between thought and emotion and how action influences action.
Instead of clinging to comfortable suppositions about yourself and
the world, continually seek the truth. Be adventurous and have
courage, for observation is the road to wisdom.

Self-Acceptance and Identity

The honesty that you need in order to observe entails acceptance
(see Chapter 6 for more about acceptance.) When observing in this
way it is not unusual to discover things that we don't like. Our first
reaction is usually to resist or deny what has come up. Each time we
resist or deny, however, we simply push our discovery underground,
ensuring that it will rise again. On the other hand, if we continue to
simply observe it, the negative charge we attach to it is gradually removed, eventually liberating us completely from our discomfort. So,

continue to observe when this happens. Don't be afraid to be honest with yourself. The hardest to observe is yourself because often what you find is the hardest to accept. To observe honestly may require that you shed old ideas about who you are and what you're like. You may uncover parts that you are ashamed of, make you sad or are hard to accept. You may find within you jealousy or greed. You may have to experience painful feelings of being unloved or unaccepted.

I know that in my own life I used to have a hard time accepting that I had anger within me. I had this image of the perfect spiritual person being somewhat like the ever-calm Buddha. "Buddha never got angry!" I said to myself. So I decided that if I was going to be a spiritual person I could never be angry, but should always try to transmute those feelings. So every time that I even started to observe anger within me, I tried to tell myself that it wasn't there, that I had transmuted it or that it was something else. It only made it worse if someone even suggested that I was angry. I would hotly deny it! The more that I pushed it away, the worse it got. For awhile, I wouldn't even allow myself to observe it at all. Finally I couldn't ignore it any longer. I slowly began to notice my anger instead of denying it. Then I began to notice how I tried to not be angry and discovered that underneath it I felt that I was somehow bad every time that I was angry, that I was unworthy, that I was unlovable.

As I continued to observe my anger and the associated under-lying emotions that I had discovered something miraculous began to occur. In time, as I continued to observe, my anger lessened until it became just one more of the emotions that I experienced from time to time. Eventually, I even gave up my internal model of a spiritual person as being one who never got angry. (It helped to recall that even Jesus got mad at the money changers in the temple and threw over their tables.) My feelings of being bad or unworthy when I got angry left me entirely.

Instead of ignoring or running away from negative feelings, observe them. Let them exist within you and allow yourself to experience them as coming and going within you. Then their negative charge will lessen. You will know without a doubt that they are not who you are inside, but are only temporary feelings. If you experience difficulty accepting the negative things or "shadow side" of yourself, it will help to contemplate this:

*ENLIGHTENMENT IS NOT ABOUT BECOMING
A PERFECT HUMAN BEING,
BUT ONLY ABOUT BECOMING
PERFECTLY HUMAN.*

*IS IT NOT SAID WE ARE MADE
IN THE IMAGE OF GOD?*

It is not only negative things that are hard to accept. Sometimes positive things are equally hard. For instance, beautiful women often reject their beauty, thinking that it attracts others to their body rather than to their Self. Observe yourself impartially, accepting the entire truth as you are experiencing it in the ever-changing present moment.

Self-acceptance doesn't mean that you never change any emotions or other parts of yourself. It only means that during the time that you are in the state of observation you accept everything. After you observe, you can decide to make changes or not. In fact, it's not advisable to make any changes unless you've first spent some time observing openly and honestly, so that you can know what changes to make. Anything less will be ineffective. If you do make changes, you observe yourself deciding to change, then observe yourself making the change.

When you observe, you eventually develop a sense of identity that is apart from your mind and emotions. You become identified with you the observer, rather than with what part of yourself you are observing. When you get angry, for example, instead of being only aware of being angry, you will be the one also watching the anger. It is as if you say to yourself: "Ah, here is anger, now here is my voice being raised, here is guilt for feeling anger, here is clenching in my stomach, here is the wanting to strike out, here is the feeling of hurt and sadness," etc. Instead of mistaking yourself as *being* the anger (and the associated reactions), you are just *having* it. The more you observe, the more you are aware of yourself as the ever-steady one (the observer) upon whose surface these endless thoughts and emotions come and go.

With less personal involvement and more knowledge of the workings of your mind and emotions, you will experience them differently. You will still feel and think, but it won't seem so critical or pressing. With less personal investment, your fear won't last as long or be as intense. Your sadness will pass more quickly. You won't desperately cling to temporary feelings of ecstasy, relying instead on the deeper happiness within that is now allowed to naturally emerge. As your thoughts and feelings cease to imprison you, this sense of yourself deepens into a wordless and formless clarity. You develop a rich calmness, and an unexplainable yet peaceful sense of identity that has nothing to do with the "passing show" of things observed. With that consciousness, a deep inner happiness will begin to grow within your heart.

Practicing Observation During Everyday Life

This practice of observation is perfect for a busy lifestyle because, as explained earlier, there is no end to what can be observed. When you are outside, observe nature. See how the wind turns the leaves as it rustles through the trees. Notice the delicate balance and interdependencies of all animals, plants, people, the earth and sky, seeing how the altering of one part affects the rest. If you're doing dishes, observe the food leaving the plates, feel the soapy water on your hands, be aware of the feeling of the dishrag and the action of scrubbing on the plates. If you are getting a cup of tea or cooking a meal, observe every detail of each action, every smell and taste sensation from beginning to end. Observe every detail of each object involved. The old familiar teapot, for example, looks different every time you view it. The light reflects differently off its surface every time that you hold it. The beads of moisture dripping down its sides form different patterns as they flow downward. The tea leaves at the bottom of the pot form different patterns every time.

The rest of your life holds so much more when you start to observe. With observation, even the most mundane things in life become meaningful and interesting. Your entire viewpoint shifts. Life becomes your ally rather than your enemy, because each happening in it, however threatening or insignificant, becomes an opportunity to gain wisdom. Life becomes a journey of discovery rather than something that must be endured or conquered. The practice of observing helps us to let go of fear and insecurity, to relax, and embrace every part of our lives.

Observe and see how much your world is determined by your own thoughts and feelings. Have you noticed how ugly the world seems, for example, when you're in a bad mood? Similarly, have you noticed how wonderful the world seems when you're "in love?" With observation you will ultimately see that your thoughts and feelings create "realities" in the world, and even of yourself, which are really just illusions. What's more, with this revelation we see that we can have a choice about how we experience our lives.

Observation Meditation
(Observing Your Thoughts)

The following meditation is one with many far-reaching benefits. Some of these are: You will learn to observe. Your ability to

ll improve as you learn to focus on one thought
listracted by others. Your mind will become clear and
strong. You will feel your mind, body and emotions calm as you
become more present-centered. You'll feel less anxiety, fear and
tension. You'll begin to feel lighter, as if all your burdens are falling
from your shoulders. Your inner strength will begin to emerge,
leaving you feeling free and clear. Most importantly, this meditation
has the potential to lead you to the ever-present Self, the spiritual
essence that exists independently from your thoughts or emotions.

These benefits will not come to you all at once. When you first
start doing this meditation, you may experience nothing more than a
momentary calm within you. Or you may at first experience your
mind racing more than ever. You might have trouble sitting still and
concentrating. If these things happen, don't worry. The more you do
this meditation, the easier it gets. Don't try to force the changes you
want. This not only won't work, but it will have the opposite effect
that you desire. This is an ancient Buddhist practice that has worked
for centuries. In fact, it is said that this meditation alone can lead you
all the way to the enlightenment that you seek. Anyone who practices this meditation faithfully finds it will work. Patience and per-
sistence is the key.

The Meditation

1. Choose a place and time to do this meditation where
   you will not be interrupted until after you are finished.

2. Sit in a chair with your spine straight, your feet flat on
    the floor, and your hands resting on your lap. Your
    head should be looking straight ahead; your chin
    should be level. If you like, you can lie flat on your
    back on a firm surface. Choose the position above that
    is the most comfortable for you.

3. Close your eyes and begin to focus on your breathing.
    Breathe in through your nose with a long, slow, deep
    breath. Be aware of the air as it enters through your
    nose and flows downward to fill your lungs. When your
    lungs are filled, slowly breathe outward. Be aware as the
    air passes out from your nose to completely empty your
    lungs. At no time should you strain or gasp for air.
    Continue this process, relaxing and centering yourself
    with every out-breath. Do this for one minute. If you
    are still not relaxed, do it for up to three minutes.

4. Now, begin to breathe normally, and shift your focus
    to your thoughts. Begin to paying closer attention to
    what you are thinking. If you have trouble finding
    any thoughts, find the voice inside you that may be
    saying, "What thoughts? I'm not having any
    thoughts." Focus on that.

5. Now continue to observe your thoughts as they arise. Watch each thought as it comes. Continue to observe as it departs. When that thought is gone, drop your attention from it and focus on the next thought that arises. If you cannot drop your attention from a departing thought, just observe yourself thinking it again.

6. Don't deliberately try to think. Just be patient, and let thoughts come up in their own time and manner, and then focus on them as they come up.

7. Watch one thought lead to another. Watch partial thoughts as well as complete thoughts. Let thoughts come up as they may. Don't repress thoughts or judge yourself. Don't stop to analyze your thoughts. If the next thought that arises, however, is a judgment or analysis of the last thought, observe it too. Watch all thoughts, even those you may not like or understand.

8. Eventually, you will find that your mind has slowed down. Instead of thoughts racing from one to another, they arise more slowly. You may become aware of spaces or lulls between your thoughts. When that happens, observe the space between your thoughts until another thought arises.

9. Anytime you find your mind wandering, bring your
    focus back to your thoughts again.

10. If you catch yourself being distracted by other emo-
    tions or other outside sounds and disturbances, just
    drop your attention from them and focus again on
    your thoughts.

11. At times you may be distracted by many inner sensa-
    tions such as sounds, colors or lights. You may have
    sensations of floating or flying. Don't let yourself be
    distracted by these sensations. Drop your attention
    from them if they arise, and focus, instead on your
    thoughts again.

12. At times you may find that your body involuntarily
    rocks back and forth, or makes other motions. You
    may find that your breathing speeds up or slows down.
    You may find that your breathing stops entirely. These
    are all natural processes and may happen as you do
    this meditation. If you find yourself distracted by this,
    just focus on your thoughts again. Observe those
    thoughts that are focused on what is happening to
    your body or breathing.

13. When you are done with the meditation, shift your focus away from your thoughts and back to your breathing. Inhale deeply and quickly through your nose, and exhale forcefully through your mouth. Do this three times. Then feel the chair or floor beneath you. Recall the room or environment in which you are doing this meditation.

14. When you are ready, open your eyes. Then stretch your body, and get up.

You can start doing this meditation for as little as three minutes at a time. Then slowly increase your time. In order to begin to experience the benefits of this meditation, do it every day for at least thirty days. As you become more practiced, you can apply the things you've learned here in your daily routine. No matter where you are, short of driving your car, you can close your eyes for a few moments, relax and watch your thoughts. Any time that you feel anxious or too overrun with thoughts, or you need clarity of mind, do this meditation for a few moments or as long as you need.

If you don't immediately experience everything that is in these instructions, don't worry. Everyone will have their own unique experience when doing this meditation. Nor is there any right or wrong experience to have. The only thing that matters is to focus on your thoughts, practice consistently and allow time for the full benefits to emerge.

Go Ahead...Lift Up The Mask.
Peer Into The Dark Corners
Of Yourself
And Be Surprised.

You Aren't Who You Were Afraid
You Might Be.

And You Are
Who You Were Afraid
You Might Not Be.

CHAPTER FOUR

Remember

The Third Practice

"*R*emember—and the Way will be shown to
you." These words capture the essence of
the third practice, which is so vitally important
on the path to enlightenment and self-discovery.
As we will be using the term here, remembering
means connecting with Higher Spirit, which is
manifest throughout the universe in every form of
life, including our own. Although the Higher
Spirit has no form, occupies no particular space,
and is beyond any logical conception or explanation, we all carry the knowledge of it within us,
and it is this we seek to remember. This is true
even when we have rejected the more traditional

notions of God, or don't even consider ourselves
religious or spiritual. If you think back in your
life, you'll probably find you've experienced Higher
Spirit in peak experiences, in your sexuality,
while running or exercising, or when "falling in
love." If you're a mother you may have had this
experience when birthing your child. Many have
experienced this special presence out in nature,
perhaps on a deserted beach, a mountain top or
in the empty expanse of desert. Even times when
we are faced with incredible danger we sometimes
experience this Higher Spirit.

Many times when we experience this Higher Spirit it feels like a
force that is greater than all the world's madness combined. Though
it can feel infinitely larger than you, it also seems familiar and personal. Many people say that when they are *not* remembering this
Spirit, they long for it, as one might long for home.

You can remember this formless Spirit by assigning it a word
or image. Instead of Higher Spirit, the word Truth may have more
meaning for you, or Love, Ultimate Reality, Inner Self or Higher
Self, Soul, God, Yaweh, Jehovah, Guru, Rama or Spirit. Bear in
mind, however, that the word or image is just the vehicle to help you
remember the experience of the Higher Spirit. The particular word
you use to describe the Higher Spirit doesn't matter, only the experience does.

While remembering will lead you to the experience of the
Spirit within you, it does much more. Each time you remember and

reach out for the Spirit, the Spirit reaches for you at the same time. You forge a pathway where you and the Higher Spirit meet in joyous reunion. In this mystical meeting you finally merge with your true inner Beloved. Here you will find your true Self and the inner strength that will support you through all adversity.

This spiritual truth has been expressed throughout time in most spiritual texts and in many diverse traditions. It has been spoken of as the "grace of God," the "divine miracle," a blessing, or the "down-pouring of the Holy Spirit." There is an ancient symbol that is used both in the Jewish and Hindu religions to express this two-way path. In the Jewish tradition it is called the Seal of Solomon, or the Jewish Star. In the Hindu tradition it is the symbol of the heart center. This six-sided star consists of two triangles. One triangle points down, symbolizing Spirit coming to man. The other triangle points up, symbolizing man coming to Spirit. Sometimes a small dot is added in the center called the *bindu*. This symbolizes the heart center where Spirit and man are one.

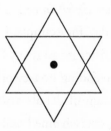

It is appropriate that this symbol is for the heart center, for this path joining God and man, Spirit and matter, duality and oneness, is not a path of the intellect, not something you can figure out. It is the path of the internal Self, a path of the soul. It is in the heart that this path is formed and the Higher Spirit is known because the essence of the Higher Spirit is love. Remember the Higher Spirit and each time that you do, relax, let your heart be open and build your pathway a little more.

Each time you remember the Higher Spirit, you receive an inner blessing. You'll feel an in-pouring of love, inner peace and comfort. You'll feel refreshed, energized and inspired. Sometimes these "gifts from the Spirit" shake you to your core with their awesome magnificence. Other times they may touch you ever so slightly, barely registering in your consciousness, only delicately whispering their presence in your heart and mind.

The Experience of Remembering

We can remember Higher Spirit in any situation and under any circumstances. The other day, for example, I was driving the kids to school, feeling like I was frittering away my life in the daily grind of endless errands, the never-ending housework, a constantly ringing telephone, and the mountain of details associated with running a business. I started feeling overwhelmed and upset, feeling that the true purpose of my life was being buried beneath all this "stuff." Instead of letting myself get depressed, angry or overwhelmed, I started repeating a name for the Higher Spirit that I use.

Gradually, I felt better. I felt a surge of lightness flow through me, and I could see my life at that point differently than I was viewing it just minutes before. I saw the incredible service that I was performing just in providing a loving home for my kids. I saw the expansive business and home environments that were created just by being conscious. I saw the true effect one conscious life can have just in the course of living day to day. I saw how the love that I gave my children could be passed on for generations, eventually affecting perhaps many hundreds of people. It was as if I was lifted up to see again my true purpose that had temporarily been buried from my sight. I didn't have to be doing "grand" things in my life to be valuable. As I saw this, my heart opened and I experienced a flooding of love and thankfulness. I began singing. Once again I was given proof of how well it works to just remember the Higher Spirit. It doesn't have to require hours of formal practice or meditation.

Does this mean that each time you remember the Higher Spirit you'll feel ecstatic, or will immediately know the answers to all your problems? No, it doesn't. Each time that you remember, the experience is different. But each time that you remember, the Higher Spirit visits you, whether you are conscious of it or not. Usually, however, the more that you have experienced the Higher Spirit in your life, the more you will detect its presence as it comes to you. No matter how aware you are of it, it leaves its enduring impression in your consciousness.

When remembering, don't *expect* anything to happen. That will limit your experience of the Spirit's presence, but that's not really the point. Rather, the purpose is to bring the Higher Spirit continually into your consciousness. Finally, remembering also helps you to keep up the other spiritual practices. Just remember, and then do whatever of the other five practices feels appropriate to you at the time. If nothing else, use the remembrance of Spirit as a practice in itself.

Visual, Environmental and Musical Reminders

In a busy, modern lifestyle, it is very easy to forget all about Spirit. There seem to be so many immediate things to handle that the entire day can slip by before you even think of anything else but the immediate tasks involved with your kids, your work, your lover or spouse, and your own feelings. Who has time to remember with so many other things that seem so pressing? There is so much to distract you that you simply forget.

In order to remember Spirit during the course of our busy lives, it's helpful to have reminders. The first method for reminding us to remember is to set up visual reminders that give you a sense of the spiritual. Hang pictures of things that inspire you, like a beautiful sunrise, a single rose, or a newborn baby. Or hang pictures of great saints, people who have been teachers to you or pictures of places or activities that recall moments when you felt the touch of Spirit.

My husband and I joke that these reminders seem to continually sprout up all over our home and in our yard. At last count, we had fifty-two "reminders!" Everywhere we look we have some type of representation of the Spirit—constantly reminding us to remember. Rather than being obtrusive, however, they're subtle. If a person came into our home who wasn't particularly spiritually oriented, the pictures and statues and other things would seem to be our art collection or a gathering of interesting things from nature.

Pictures aren't the only visual reminders. We also set clear quartz crystals around to remind us of the diamond-like perfection of the True Reality. We use amethyst and rose quartz stones to remind us of healing and love. We set out shells to remind us of the unending coming and going of the ocean waves, of infinity and open space. Finally, we usually wear something special, a piece of jewelry or clothing that reminds us of Spirit. Many people like to wear special jewelry or carry an amulet, stone or other small object in their pocket to feel during the day.

Have your environment be as spiritually elevating as possible. You might want to fill your home with scents that uplift you. If the woods are particularly inspiring for you, have pine scent in the air. If you have worked with Eastern spiritual methods, sandalwood incense may help you remember. If the Native American teachings have meaning for you, burn sage, sweetgrass or cedar. Each scent has its own particular effect on the consciousness. Experiment with different scents and find one that appeals to you.

Bring beauty to your home or work environment, keeping your living and work spaces as clean and uncluttered as possible. (This will help you to be more inwardly calm and peaceful.) Decorate with flowers or green houseplants. Paint your walls with what are uplifting, heartful colors for you and for your family. Open your blinds and let in the sunlight, and if it's warm enough, open your windows and bring in the fresh air. Try turning off the TV and turning on some music. Then let the growing peacefulness and inspiration in your work and home environment help create the peace and inspiration within you that will remind you of the true reality within.

Music can have a particularly inspiring effect on consciousness, so try using it in the background while you work, meditate or simply relax. Everyone has their own taste in music, of course. Ours includes classical music of the baroque era which we find calming as it lightly cavorts through fugal and contrapuntal melodies. Bach preludes are good examples of this style. Other classical music, such as Pachelbel's *Canon in D* is increasingly used for restful inspiration. *The Four Seasons* by Vivaldi is also excellent. Try romantic favorites such as *Clair de Lune* by Debussy, *Liebestraum No. 3 in A flat major* by Franz Liszt, Mendelssohn's *Song Without Words in E major,* Chopin's *Etude in E major* or Schumann's *Traumerei.* The music of Mozart is also excellent.

Many people like New Age music, finding it calming, meditative and inspiring. Try listening to Robert Gass's *Om Namaha Sivaya, Shri Ram,* or *From the Goddess.* Brian Eno's music, *Ambient #1: Music For Airports* and *The Pearl* is extraordinarily peaceful and meditative. The music by Deuter is delightfully inspiring. Recordings of nature sounds that are excellent as ambient background music for work, meditation, and relaxation.

There are also guided meditation recordings that are useful to relax, heal, inspire and open your heart. I have recorded both music and guided visualizations with music background designed to open your heart, lift you up into the celestial realms, and gently relax you, creating peace in your soul. *Watergarden* and my newest recording, *Voyager*, are particularly inspiring music recordings, while *Relax* and *Healing* are two guided visualization recordings with *Love* expected to be released in 1994 (ordering information in back of book). Whatever you listen to, just relax and let go—let yourself be carried by the sounds back to your inner Self.

Ceremonies

Ceremonies are another excellent way to remember the Higher Spirit. These usually have to be arranged or scheduled and so aren't as easily done just in the course of your daily living. They can be very effective, however, to give you some special time apart from your daily routine in order to remember the Higher Spirit. The most obvious ceremony is to go to church or to the temple. Try different types of temples or churches to see if you can find one that you like. If you don't want to participate in a traditionally religious ceremony, you can create your own.

Mini-ceremonies can be done anywhere at anytime. Perhaps you can find a special spot outdoors where you can sit for an hour every Sunday or Saturday morning and contemplate, pray, sing or just sit in silence. If you have a family, you can all sit together. Or choose one time during the week to build a fire in your fireplace and meditate in front of it.

Contemplate the wood burning, imagining that as the wood burns away, so do the limitations and barriers that keep you away from your inner truth. Each time that you pass into your house, for example, you can touch the doorstep and say to yourself, "I touch the feet of the Higher Spirit." When you hang up the phone after speaking to someone, you can lay your palm on your heart center in the middle of your chest and say to yourself, "Together we are joined in the love of our inner Spirit." As you dress yourself, you can say, "I am not my body, but the true reality within." Once you have created a ceremony, however, do it regularly so that it can become automatic and thus build in its power to remind you of the Spirit.

Repeating a Name
For the Higher Spirit

One of the most effective ways to remember the Higher Spirit is to constantly repeat the name that you associate with it. In fact, this way is so effective that it has been described as a complete path in itself. This method can also be done anywhere, anyplace, and during any activity. It requires nothing except your intention.

In many traditional Eastern spiritual practices, teachers give their students "mantras," that is, special words, sounds or images to hold in the mind to remind the student to remember. The mantra can alter your consciousness to ultimately lead to the realization of God. This ancient science, called jappa yoga, nad or mantra yoga, is as effective today as it was centuries ago. Western spiritual traditions also have their own specially charged words, some of which are given below. The following is a short list of mantras that you may want to try:

1. RAMA - (sounds like rah - mah), or RAM - (sounds like rahm). This is the word associated with the heart center. It is said to bring love and compassion into your life as it opens your heart. Both Ram and Rama are ancient Hindu names for God. In the ancient Hindu scriptures, Rama was a prince who was the perfect embodiment of the golden light of God.

2. OM - (sounds like ohm as in home). This sound is said to be the primal sound of the universe. It is often associated with the third eye center and spiritual wisdom. (Sometimes it is pronounced AUM, with the slight sound of ah preceding the om.)

3. OM RAM - (sounds like ohm - rahm). This combines the qualities of both Ram and Om.

4. AVE MARIA - (sounds like ah-vay mah-ree-ah). This brings the qualities of compassion and forgiveness and opens the heart center. It also will also help

you to realize the feminine, mothering nature of the Spirit. Maria refers to Mary, the mother of Jesus.

5. YAWEH - (sounds like yah-way). This is a name for God associated with the ancient Cabalistic or Judaic traditions. It will help to open your heart center of compassion and the mystical understandings of your third eye.

6. WAHE GURU - (sounds like wah-hay goo-roo). This is a Sikh word meaning "Hail to the great, glorious inner teacher," or "God is great." The sounds in these words open your heart center and your third eye, and activate your ability to communicate and speak the truth.

8. EK ONG KAR - (sounds like eck - ohng - car). (Eck is pronounced as in the word "neck." Ohng is pro- nounced with the ng sound in the back of the throat as in the word "lung.") These words mean "there is one God," meaning that there is only one underlying reality from which all life's appearances and manifes- tations stem. These words lead you to the realization of the reality beyond all form.

9. OM NAMAH SIVAYA - (sounds like ohm-nahmah-shee-vie (as in pie)-yah). This means "I bow to Shiva." Shiva is an ancient Hindu name of God. This refers to the aspect of God that is golden and firelike as the sun. Shiva is the destroyer aspect of God, or that part of us and all life that dies to be born again.

10. SAT NAM - (sounds like saht-nahm). This is a Sikh mantra that means "Gods name is Truth." This refers to the formless aspect of God that can be best be experienced within us as that which is the most true or real. This also opens up the heart center of love and compassion and balances the male and female energies in the body.

11. AMEN - (sounds like ah-main). This expresses the thankfulness that is felt when the Higher Spirit is experienced and opens the heart center.

These are just a few words that you may want to try. If you have another word for the Higher Spirit that you are more comfortable with, use that. The most important thing to remember when repeating any name, is that it only represents the Higher Spirit and is not the Higher Spirit itself. So there is no need to insist that one word is more correct than another. What is important is what will work for you, and what works for you might not work for the next person.

When you choose one of these specially-charged words that appeals to you, repeat it silently or out loud. It is important when repeating this word to also listen to it. Relax and let yourself be carried by its sound. Feel its vibrations in your throat, mouth and body. Repeat your mantra or special word for the Higher Spirit throughout the day, no matter what you're doing. Say it silently, aloud, or even sing it. Repeat it as you're falling asleep at night. Sometimes you'll be able to even say it in your dreams. At first it may be hard to remember to repeat your mantra. You'll forget many times during the day. With time, however, it will become automatic.

When selecting one of these mantras, chose the one that just appeals to you for no special reason and repeat it for thirty days. After thirty days, which is the time it takes for it to start doing its work, you can try another. Eventually you'll find one that seems right for you or has the best appeal.

If none of these specially charged words appeal to you, you might try one of the following sentences as reminders. Repeat it just as you would the others. Though these words are not specially charged like some of the ancient mantras, many people find them invaluable for remembering Spirit.

1. I am Spirit, and Spirit is me.

2. All that I see is Spirit.

3. Dearly Beloved, I'm Yours.

4. I open my heart to Thee.

5. Thank you, thank you, thank you.

6. Love is all there is.

7. You are present in all I see, all I do and all I am.

8. I am love.

Remembering to Repeat Your Mantra

At first it may seem difficult to remember to repeat your mantra or specially chosen word(s) for the Higher Spirit. If that is the case, here are some things that can help you: First, your own breathing can serve as a reminder. Breathe naturally, and each time that you breathe in, say the entire word that you have chosen, one part of the word, or one syllable. When you breathe out, say the entire word again, the rest of the word or another syllable. If you are saying the word AMEN, for example, say the first syllable "A" on the in-breath, and the second syllable "MEN" on the out-breath. If you're saying the mantra, OM NAMAH SIVAYA, say the words "OM NAMAH" on the in-breath and the word SIVAYA on the out-breath.

Next, use the never-ending rhythms of life in your workplace, in your home and out in nature to help you remember to repeat your special name for the Higher Spirit. Notice these life rhythms and chant along with them. If you pay attention, all of your daily life is filled with different rhythms. Silently say your mantra along with f the clock, or in time with the music on your radio.

in your car, hear the drone of the car wheels as OM.

Even your own body movements can help you. Say one word or phrase of your specially charged word each time your feet meet the ground when you walk or run. Repeat your mantra along with your own heartbeat.

In my own life, I remember many days at the beach playing frisbee with my children. As I drew back my arm to throw the frisbee, I'd say "RA" to myself, then when I threw it I'd say "MA". When I caught the frisbee I'd repeat RAMA. I tried to focus entirely on the mantra instead of any other thoughts. It made a wonderful practice —and we all had fun!

The Farmer and the Spiritual Man

*E*ven with the best of intentions, you may only remember to repeat your mantra once or twice a day. Don't despair, even that is effective. There is an old story about this. According to this story, once there was a very spiritual man who lived in retreat and did nothing but meditate, pray and remember to repeat the name of God all day. At the same time, living next door was a farmer who worked from dawn to late at night taking care of his farm and his family. Every once in a while the farmer remembered to say God's name. Sometimes it was two or three times a day, sometimes it was only once a day, or once every other day. Both men died and went to heaven. The spiritual man was walking through heaven and happened to see his old neighbor there. The spiritual man became angry at this. "What is this farmer doing here? He was busy in his fields all day, not remembering God, while I was remembering God and repeating his name all day!" The spiritual man was so upset by this that he went to complain to God. After hearing his complaint, God replied: "The farmer has earned his right to be here even more than you. After all, you had lots of time to remember Me. You had nothing else to do but dwell on Me all day and night. This man, however, had many responsibilities and no time at all to remember Me. How much more valuable, then, was each time that he repeated my name than the thousands of times you did!"

This story doesn't mean that we shouldn't try to remember the Higher Spirit. It only means that we should know that each time we do remember, it is important and valuable.

Meditation To Remember
The Higher Spirit

The following meditation can be done whenever you want to remember the Higher Spirit. It can be done for a few moments anywhere or anyplace, or can be done as a daily practice. It is said that this meditation, alone, can carry you to enlightenment. It also will help you open your heart so that you can experience compassion, love and empathy. It will lead you to deep experiences of inner peace and extraordinary calm. It is excellent when experiencing anxiety, for it will slow down your racing thoughts and emotions, providing mental and emotional clarity. You will be able to perfectly concentrate your mind at will.

In this meditation you repeat the name for the Higher Spirit, RAMA. Rama, in the ancient vedic scripture called the "Ramayana," was the princely ruler of the ancient, golden city of Ayodya. There are many stories of Rama's exploits, all revealing his unwavering love for the Higher Spirit, his honesty, his courage, and his sense of service and duty. Rama is the epitome of one who is enlightened, Spirit and man perfectly merged in loving service of both heaven and earth. Truth forms the core of his courage, and the golden light of divine awareness illuminates his heart, radiating gloriously for all to see.

RAMA also has another meaning. RA represents the warming heat and raw energy of the golden sun. MA represents the cool, peaceful light of the silver moon. RA is male, yang energy, charging forward, rocket-like, bright and bold. MA is female, yin energy, enveloping, cool and subtle. When you repeat RAMA, you balance the male/female energies in your body. You balance the logical/intuitive mind. You balance all of yourself so that you rest in the peace of perfect equilibrium. When you are thus balanced, you make room for Higher Spirit to enter you and speak to your soul. It is only when your body, mind and heart are at rest that you can begin to walk in joyful freedom from all fear, doubt and limitation.

While this meditation is obviously not intended to be done "on the run," it is important because it prepares you for the shorter exercises designed to be done while you are involved in other activities.

The longer, more intense practices train your mind so that even in the midst of major distractions, such as a noisy work place, you can easily do your shorter practices and receive the peace of mind they provide. After doing this meditation, the RAMA mantra will be so much a part of you that it will be easy to repeat it silently during your day.

The Meditation

1. Sit upright, with your spine straight, both feet on the ground, your hands resting in your lap with your palms facing up. Touch the tips of your thumbs to the tips of your first (index) fingers. (This hand position, called *gyan mudra*, is said to bring wisdom.) If you like, you can sit in the lotus or half-lotus yoga position. Even though you are sitting upright, you should be relaxed. If you cannot sit upright in a relaxed manner, sit with your back supported by an upright chair.

2. Hold your head straight, facing forward, with your chin dropped down slightly (about an inch). When your chin is dropped the right amount you will feel the back of your neck stretching slightly upward as if elongating. This will help open your throat center, the center of communication.

3. Close your eyes, bringing your focus to your heart center in the middle of your chest.

4. As you focus on your heart center, become aware of your breathing (breathe normally).

5. Now, as you breathe in, mentally repeat the sound RA. Feel as if the breath and the sound RA enters and fills your heart center.

6. When you breathe out, mentally repeat the sound MA. Feel as if the breath and the sound MA leave from your heart center.

7. Maintain your focus on the sounds RAMA entering and leaving your heart center. If your attention wanders, just bring it back to your heart center and continue to repeat RAMA.

8. If you feel any tension, let yourself imagine it leaving you as you breathe out. Relax with every out-breath. As you do this, however, don't drop your attention from your repetition of RAMA.

9. You may experience many different emotions,
    thoughts and other sensations during the course of
    this meditation. No matter what they are, or how
    terrible or wonderful they seem, don't let them distract
    you. If you find that you are paying attention to these
    sensations, drop your attention, and bring it back to
    your heart center with the repetition of RAMA.

10. If it seems difficult at first to focus your mind continu-
    ally on RAMA as it enters and leaves your heart
    center, remind yourself that this is a natural part of the
    meditation process. The more you meditate the easier
    it will get.

11. Do this meditation for three minutes at first. When
    you feel ready, increase your time to seven minutes,
    then eleven minutes. You can do this for thirty
    minutes, then an hour. There is no harm in doing this
    meditation for even lengthier periods of time.

13. Eventually, RAMA will seem to repeat itself through
    you. RAMA will become as natural to you as your
    own breathing. It is even said that if you repeat
    RAMA as you are dying, it will carry you past all fear,
    into the golden light of the Higher Spirit.

AWAKENING

Ah, sweet Truth, fierce demanding One,
     unspoken longings trapped in my
     heart call for you.
A living flame of remembrance
     pleads for awakening.
Beloved, set my soul free!

With your Name upon my lips,
     I open my heart
     and beg you to consume me
     upon your golden pyre of love.
I sacrifice myself to your mercy,
     for I cry for release.

Your Name in my soul,
     I leap, diving headlong,
     falling into your
     abyss of not-knowing,
     as you circle me
     in your fiery embrace.

I surrender to your burning.
And even as I writhe
in unbearable anguish,
I pray from the depth of my longing,
burn me...consume me,
to the core of my reality.

Serpent-like your heat
rages up my spine,
and explodes my mind
into glorious shards
of living brightness.
My darkness is shattered to light.

Wildly, gleefully I dance
in your merciful and healing flames,
spinning my pain to pleasure.
For I have died only to be born.
I rise transmuted, phoenix-like,
from the ashes of my self-imposed
bondage.

With my body now radiant sunlight
and my eyes glowing embers,
with starlight my crown
and lightning my scepter,
I ride the wings of my victorious heart,
and sing aloud your sweet song of
freedom.

CHAPTER FIVE

Let Truth Guide Your Way

The Fourth Practice

*L*et the truth that is within you, in every
other being, and in all of life, guide your
way—and the way will be constantly revealed to
you. This is the essence of the fourth practice. Be
who you really are, live in a state of constant
Truth and you will find your answers within.
When you have decided to lead this kind of life,
living moment-to-moment in the present, observing what is truly so, apart from any reliance on
what should be, could be or is supposed to be, it
is as if your internal slate is wiped clean, waiting
to be written anew—every moment created with
truth's "pen." The Zen Buddhists refer to this as

the "beginner's mind." Have a beginner's mind
that is as clear and present-centered as a young
child's, and then follow Truth's directions as im-
peccably as you are able. Become a warrior for
the truth, letting nothing stand in your way—not
other people, and not even your own egotistic
desires and preferences. This is the way to
wisdom.

Truth Versus
Relative Reality

All ideas that people have about reality seem to be relative to their own culture, beliefs and past experiences. Everyone sees and hears differently—even when looking at the same event. There is an old story that speaks of this phenomena and teaches us to question what we mean when we speak of Truth: Three blind men were trying to describe an elephant. One blind man felt the elephant's leg and said, "Oh, the elephant is as big around as my waist, is taller than my head, and has a flat bottom to it." The other blind man felt the trunk of the elephant and said "No, an elephant is long and thin, with a hole at the end that seems to be its mouth." The third blind man felt the elephant's ear and said, "No, you are both mistaken. The elephant actually is flat and thin, with little hairs over it, and it makes a flapping motion." All of the men were *relatively* right, but no one truly discovered what the entire elephant actually looked like. Life is like that. What is true for one person may not be true for another.

The truth we seek on a spiritual path is different than relative truth. It cannot be found through our five senses, our beliefs or any of our commonly held "understandings" about life. The truth we explored here refers to that indescribable something that can be known but not explained—that ultimate reality that has been described as the Higher Spirit. This truth isn't confined to the boundaries of our bodies, even though we can experience it inside us. It has no beginning or ending, nor does it have anything to do with being right or wrong.

Truth is not an idea. It doesn't change as opinions and viewpoints change. It doesn't change as we get older. You or I may change but this Truth never changes. When you discover Truth, it's as if you've found an old friend again. You have a sense of rediscovering what you had temporarily forgotten. Even if its voice within you guides you in changing directions, it is ultimately guiding you in the direction of its own realization. It's not found in books, instructions or rules, but can always be found within you if you know how to look. This is what will provide you unfailing guidance if you heed its voice.

This is not to say that this is the only truth you should pay attention to in your life. Relative truth is valid and useful in its own way. What each blind man discovered about the elephant, for example, was not false. But each man had only a portion of the truth. In fact, following the road of relative truth can lead you to the deeper

Reality. As you become more present-centered, you will find that your relative truth slowly yields to a larger truth. Be fluid, yet strong. Be like the trees. The ones that continue to live and flourish are those that are best able to bend with the wind. Continually yield to the Truth. The path that unfolds to us in this way is not about being "right;" rather it's about discerning and following truth as you experience it for yourself—moment by moment.

Learning to bend like a tree doesn't mean abandoning your own integrity. On the contrary, it means being guided by the inner guiding voice of Truth and becoming increasingly true to your own sense of personal integrity. It is only when you can yield, when you don't feel compelled to "prove" your own point of view, that you can fully embrace your own sense of personal integrity. When you let go of the need to be right, it becomes much easier to accept other truths as they are revealed to you. When you cling to your relative truth, you're forced to pretend you believe something that deep down inside, you know isn't true.

To follow the path of Truth, then, is to learn how to be guided by your own inner integrity—no matter what. This is so in the simple matters of life as well as the more important things. Go ahead, for example, and pick up that piece of paper that you dropped on the ground. Don't tell a lie just to make things easier for yourself. Don't do or say anything that feels wrong to you—even if you have to make sacrifices. Don't betray yourself. That is what it means to follow Truth.

To follow this path is to start relying more on yourself for answers. It means depending less on outer direction, whether it be your parents, your school, your spiritual teacher, your best friend or the society in which you live. Let go and trust the truth you sense inside of you. This doesn't mean that you must reject old teachings. Nor does it mean you won't have any more teachers or that you shouldn't listen to anyone. Instead, honor them for what they have taught you. No matter who or what the teaching, you must ultimately rely on your inner sense of Truth to guide you. When you do this, everything in life becomes a teacher.

What It's Like To Live In Truth

When you live in a state of Truth, it becomes both your guide and your constant reassurance. When you're present-centered, observing Truth clearly, you don't feel confused. Not only does your deep-rooted fear and sadness disappear, but also any sense of chaos. This isn't because your life is any different (although it may be), but because you understand life in a new way, one that is different than intellectual understanding. When you understand in this way, you feel protected, cared for and relaxed. You feel satisfied and free.

When you live in a state of truth, you live in harmony. You feel a deep sense of peaceful union, with other beings and with everything else. Even the terrible things in life are in harmony when you see the "larger picture." When you have this sense of being in union, you are able to see that all of life is in harmony with each and every part of itself. Parts may be pleasant to you, and parts might not—but it's still okay. To live in harmony with life means to stop fighting it, to let go and just let life happen.

This doesn't mean that you turn a blind eye to what is happening, justifying it by saying that it will all be okay. You still try to live your life skillfully, making every effort to live as well as you can. For example, if you're running a business, you still keep your eye on everything and try to make the correct decisions, because good intentions alone aren't going to balance the budget. If you're raising kids, you love them and try to take care of them as consciously as you can.

Just because you accept life and live in harmony with it, you don't have to become passive. (This is a mistake many people make.) You can still have preferences and maintain your personal boundaries. For example, if you're living in an abusive relationship, you can still leave. You don't have to just accept it in order to be spiritual. Going with the flow of life in this case may include creating a better life for yourself.

A few years ago I learned this lesson from one of my teachers. I had a dream in which two people were holding my arms and a third was digging his fist deeply into my solar plexus. It hurt tremendously, but in the dream I learned how to endure the pain and still maintain my inner peace. When I relayed this dream to my teacher and told him how I had learned to endure the pain, he looked at me and replied, "Why do that?" At that moment I realized that I could make life changes and still remain in a state of acceptance. Change, too, is a part of life. Sometimes fighting change is fighting life.

When you start "going with the flow," life stops fighting you. The environment and your life circumstances support you in ways that contribute to your growth and well-being. This may manifest in simple ways. For example, when you go places in your car, you always find a parking spot. When you're thinking about someone, they'll call. When you need something, it's there. It may manifest in more complex ways also. If I'm looking for a good dayschool for my child, for example, I'll just happen to run into the friend of someone who knows the perfect school. When I'm trying to decide whether to call this school the next day, I just happen to see a poster about it in the public library. Then I'll call. (Jung calls this synchronicity.) Or, if I get a flat tire while driving, it happens right in front of a gas station. Your whole life starts to flow along much less effortlessly— even when it's difficult. This is what it feels like to live in harmony.

A Personal Example

A few years ago I went through a period when everything that could possibly go wrong did—all at once. Just about everything that could fall apart did. I was diagnosed with pre-cervical cancer and came down with pneumonia at the same time that my marriage fell apart. As I began going through separation and divorce proceedings, I discovered that I was pregnant. At the same time, my business almost went bankrupt (losing about $20,000 a month), and I had to fire and replace almost my entire management. While I was handling this, I came down with pneumonia again, took care of my four-year old's emotional problems with the divorce, and constantly dealt with my angry and threatening ex-husband, who I feared was trying to take my children away me. As if this weren't enough, when

I gave birth to my baby that same year, there were complications and I almost bled to death. Recovery from that was difficult.

During this time I began living in a completely new home in a new environment and started a new relationship. Does this sound like enough? It did to me too! However, I was not to be let off that easily. The new man in my life had a business that was also in trouble. We both ran out of money—completely. At the same time, he was renting to a tenant who had a nervous breakdown, bought shotguns, and was calling us a couple times a week threatening to kill our family. This all happened in the space of a year and a half. It got to be so much to handle that it almost became laughable. All I could do was trust what I had learned—when you follow the guiding hand of Truth, everything is as it should be, and will turn out well for everyone involved.

Using the techniques in this book, I felt inwardly peaceful, secure and deeply satisfied. I continually listened to the inner voice of Truth and found my way through all these difficulties. I could see the path that I was to take very clearly, and I did what needed to be done. At times I felt angry. At other times I cried. But I didn't lose myself, or drown in my troubles. Even though it wasn't easy, deep down inside I knew that this was all just passing, that everything was okay. With that attitude, it felt as if this was a time of problem-solving rather than a time of crisis. Because I was able to trust the deep inner Truth inside, and know that everything had a reason, and remember that none of this reflected who I really was inside, I was able to remain inwardly joyful. Even then I had a sense that my life had a certain harmony to it.

Just as promised in every spiritual teaching, following the voice of inner Truth works. Everyone was eventually happier and better off. My ex-husband is no longer angry, and is very happily married to a woman that is much better for him. I'm happily re-married and my children are both well-adjusted and happy. The renter who had the mental breakdown finally moved back to his mother's home and recovered. I was able to heal myself completely, and both our businesses are doing better than ever. For me, this was the final proof that these techniques that I had been practicing and teaching for years really work in the everyday world, and not only in the protective environment of the ashram or monastery where I had spent so many years earlier.

How to Start Living A Life of Truth

To start living a life in alignment with Truth, you need to recover your inner Self. To do this, you need to take responsibility for yourself and your life choices. Instead of believing that you're helpless, instead of only reacting as things happen to you, you can get back in the "driver's seat" of your life.

You can get back into the "driver's seat" by paying attention to how you have defined what's "normal" in your life. Ask yourself who you consider to be normal. Who are your authorities? Who gives them that power in your life? Contemplate that question honestly and you will find that you've always decided who or what you wanted to believe or follow. You made others into authority figures. This is true of us all, even when we're openly rebelling against those figures.

This is not to say that you did the wrong thing. Many times, the best thing to do it to follow something or someone. You may have had good reasons, given who you were and what stage of your development you were in. Many times it's just easier to do what everyone else is doing. Other times, you do need to learn from others by obeying them or following in their footsteps. A three-year-old child needs to learn from her parents, for example. You do need a teacher to show you a spiritual pathway if you're looking for one. But finally there comes a time to listen to the teacher within your own soul. This is the teacher that all your others have been trying to show you (if they were good teachers). No person can make you listen, however. You are the one responsible for that choice. You are the one who decides how you want to live your life. Getting back "in the driver's seat" and accepting that responsibility will lead you toward Self-recovery.

How to Hear the Inner Truth

The voice of Truth is like a sound without a sound and there is an art to hearing it. This voice of Truth is an inner knowing or an inner sense that will tell you about the reality of your experience, whether it be about yourself, other people or events in the world. You have undoubtedly heard this voice many times but didn't recognize it. For example, we often "know" when a person is lying to us even when by all outward appearances they seem to be telling the truth. And how many times have you known when a person close to you was feeling sad or angry when they insisted they were okay? Think of that "little voice" inside that gave you this information. This is the voice that you listen to. It's the voice that never makes you feel guilt or shame, only peace or love. The Quakers refer to it as the "still, quiet voice within." Some call it intuition. Some call it the guiding Spirit within.

This inner voice is an experience of knowing that can't be identified with our logical mind or our five physical senses. It seems to come from the vicinity of your heart center, in the middle of your chest, yet the more you investigate it, the more you realize that it is much larger than the boundaries of your body. It occupies no particular space and has no particular form. When you hear this inner voice it comes from within you rather than being a voice that comes from without. It is a soundless yet clear voice. It is more like an inner sense. When you hear it, it is almost as if you already know whatever it is speaking of, as if you had forgotten and now remember. There is a sense of "Oh, yes, I already know that." There is a sense of calm certainty. Yet it is not rigid as a belief often is, and it differs from thought and imagination.

Because it doesn't always seem logical or to follow cause and effect sequences, it is easy to reject this inner voice, assuming it to be invalid. However, the more seriously you take this voice, the "louder" it will speak to you. It's much like a muscle: The more you use it, the stronger it gets. When you listen to your inner voice, and follow what it tells you, you'll find the information it gives you is correct. Often you'll find that this still, quiet voice within gives you more dependable information than you can get from more logical methods of knowing. Of course, the degree of truth that this inner voice provides is determined by your ability to hear correctly.

To hear correctly, you need to be present-centered. Then you need to listen without any prejudgments. If you can observe, you can listen in this way. When you listen, have an attitude of wanting to be guided by the Higher Spirit, rather than your own egotistic desires. Have an attitude of trust.

Meditation to Develop Intuition and Hear the Inner Voice

*A*s you learn to be real, to observe, to remember *and* be present-centered, you will automatically begin to hear the inner voice. However, if you want to speed up the process, you can do the following meditation. This meditation specifically opens up what is called your "third eye," an etheric energy center located in the middle of your forehead between your two eyebrows. This center is traditionally associated with intuition, psychic abilities, creativity, and self-awareness. (This awareness of your inner voice will increase even

further if you do the yoga or meditations to open your heart c‹
given to you in Chapter 7 on meditation.) This is given as a formal
sitting meditation, however it can be done anywhere for any length
of time, whenever you feel the need to expand your viewpoint, access
creative energy, calm yourself, or hear your inner voice more clearly.

The Meditation

1. Sit in a comfortable position with your spine straight.
    If you like, you can lie on your back on the floor or
    another surface. Rest your hands on your lap or on the
    surface next to you.

2. Close your eyes and focus on the very center of your
    forehead.

3. Breathe normally through your nose and feel as if your
    breath passes in and out of the center of your forehead.

4. With each in-breath, imagine that the color royal blue
    passes in to fill your forehead. In your mind's eye, see
    only the color royal blue. If you have seeing the royal
    blue, silently say to yourself, "Royal blue fills my
    forehead."

5. With each out-breath, release any tension.

6. Next, with each in-breath, silently say the sound "OH." With each out-breath, silently say the sound "M-M-M." Let the sound "OH" flow into the sound "M-M-M" without any break.

7. If your mind wanders, just bring it back to focus on your breath, the color royal blue and the sound "OM" in and out of the center of your forehead.

8. You may begin to feel as if you are floating, or see colors or visions other than the color royal blue. If this happens, bring your attention back to the center of your forehead, your breathing, blue color and sound "OM."

9. Your breathing may automatically change in some way, either becoming very shallow or very deep. Don't try to change or alter your breathing yourself. Let your breath change by itself and continue your focus.

10. Do this for three minutes, eleven minutes, or thirty-
     one minutes at least once a day or evening. You may
     do this exercise as long as you like.

11. When you are through, take a deep breath through
     your nose, release it slowly and then open your eyes.
     Stretch your body before getting up.

12. Besides increasing your ability to hear intuitively, this
     exercise also will increase your ability to concentrate,
     calm your mind and emotions, and stimulate your
     creativity. It will help you feel whole instead of scat-
     tered and will help you feel peaceful, even when your
     life is stressful.

Balancing the Logical Mind
With the Inner Voice

In our daily lives we need to listen and act with the help of both our
inner knowing and our logical mind. There is an art to balancing
both realities so that they become mutually supportive. If you're
driving down a road and see a ball rolling into the street in front of
you, you can logically figure that someone might come running after
the ball. You can also listen to your inner voice and know, without

figuring it out, that someone is about to enter the street in front of you. By listening to both, you can avoid hitting the child who runs out after the ball.

On the other hand, if your inner voice of Truth is telling you something different than your logical mind, it is a good idea to pay attention to it. Your inner voice is always correct—as long as you can hear it correctly. For example, if your inner voice tells you that the words someone is saying are not the truth, listen to your inner voice. Chances are that it is detecting something beyond mere speech. This art of balancing the logical and intuitive develops over time and requires patience, truthfulness, courage and humility. Listen and act; if you're wrong, be willing to admit it and try again. If you're right, let this help you learn more. Either way, let both experiences continually refine your ability to hear your inner voice.

It is sometimes difficult to distinguish fanciful thinking from the true inner voice. But here are some guidelines that can help you: Fantasy carries with it an element of hope or wishful thinking; it seems to spring from the mind outward. Intuition (the inner voice) carries with it an element of quiet excitement and peace, and it seems to spring from a source beyond your mind. If you feel even the tiniest sense of disquiet, unease or dishonesty within you, chances are that you are creating your own wishful thinking, obscuring the truth of your inner voice. If you're not sure that what you're hearing is your inner voice, you're probably not hearing it.

When you hear your inner voice, there is a sense of already knowing what you're hearing. Furthermore, you feel good inside; it's as if you're in communication with yourself. (Even if it's only for a moment.) One of the best ways to become familiar with your intuitive mind is to continually test it. Honestly notice if the choices that you made while listening to your inner voice were the right ones in the "real, everyday" world. For instance, if you "heard" that you should buy a certain stock and that stock crashed as soon as you bought it, you should assume that you weren't "hearing" correctly. (I don't recommend using your "inner voice" to play the stock market however. Besides being ethically questionable, it makes more sense to more carefully investigate the companies in which you want to invest!) In other words, continually balance the information you get from your inner voice with "earthplane" reality.

Visualization to Gain Insight, Solve Problems, and Develop Effective Courses of Action

The following visualization can help you develop insight, solve problems, and discover a balanced and effective course of action based on both your logical mind and your inner voice. Besides being useful for decreasing the stress level that often accompanies major decisions in your life, it will help you discover the nature of Truth or the guiding Spirit within you.

This visualization should be done only at a time and place where you will not be interrupted until you're done. This could be as little time as ten minutes, or for as long as you like.

The Visualization

1. Sit with your spine straight and your hands resting, palms down, on the top of your legs. Your feet should be flat on the floor and your legs together. Hold your head straight, with your chin lowered slightly (one inch).

2. Close your eyes.

3. Focus your attention on your heart center, that place in the middle of your chest.

4. Take a long, slow breath through your nose and imagine that it fills your heart center. Now slowly release your breath through your nose, imagining that it leaves through the center of your chest. On the out-breath, release all physical, mental and emotional tension.

5. Do this until you are calm, clear and peaceful—as if you are a still pond of water.

6. Next, imagine that a calm violet light streams into the middle of your chest with every in-breath. Imagine that it slowly fills your body. As you continue to breathe, the violet light completely fills your body and then streams outward through the skin of your body to surround you in a glowing orb of light. (If you're having trouble imagining this, silently say to yourself, "I am completely filled with violet light which sur rounds my body in a glowing orb.")

7. With every out-breath, extend the orb or egg of purple light outward as far as you can see.

8. Next, focus your attention on the question, problem or action that you wish to view in its essence and discover the truth about.

9. State it to yourself as clearly and exactly as you can.

10. What are your thoughts about it? Let each thought come up, observe it, then let it go. Do this until you have no more thoughts about it.

11. Now, view the matter in question and see what you are feeling about it. What are your feelings? Let each feeling arise inside of you; experience it, then, let it go.

12. What happens in your body as you experience your thoughts and feelings? Observe your body and relax.

13. What do you believe about the question, problem or action on which you focus? Observe these beliefs. Can you imagine them not to be true? Can you imagine any conflicting beliefs? After you have observed each belief, let it go from your mind.

14. Focus your attention on your breath again. Take long, slow breaths in and out of the center of your chest as you did earlier. As you do this, release all physical, mental and emotional tension. Continue until you are calm, clear and peaceful as a still pond of water.

15. Move your attention to your intuitive voice, or the voice that is different from what you're thinking, believing or feeling. What does this voice say to you? Relax and listen, continually letting go of all other thoughts and emotions.

16. Hear, without having to use words.

17. Continue this process until you feel a sense of completion, fulfillment and peace inside.

18. What actions can you take that will be in alignment with this inner sense of fulfillment?

19. What new viewpoints or ideas can you have that are in alignment with this inner sense?

20. Verbalize to yourself the thoughts, feelings, ideas or realizations that you have that are in alignment with this sense of inner fulfillment.

21. Next, focus your attention back to your heart center in the middle of your chest. Breathe as if your breath travels in and out of your heart center. Do this three times.

22. Now, shift your attention back to the violet field of light which surrounds you.

23. Inhale through your nose three times, and imagine that the violet light pulls more into your body each time that you inhale. On the third breath, the violet light is entirely within you.

24. Now, breathe in and out three more times and on each in-breath, the violet light travels inward to fill your heart. On your third in-breath, your heart is entirely filled with violet light.

25. Shift your attention from your heart center to your breath. Take a deep breath in through your nose and forcibly exhale through your mouth, blowing outward. Do this three times, blowing more forcibly from your mouth each time that you blow outward.

26. Focus your attention on the chair beneath you and visualize the room or environment in which you sit. When you feel like it, open your eyes and stretch your body.

27. If you like, record what it is that you have learned, decided or realized, so that you can remember.

Your Commitment to Truth Must Be Total

Your commitment to Truth must be total. Although there are some general guidelines (see Chapter 9), there are no absolute rules by which you must act. Just look deeply within to discover what your own inner voice is telling you. Uncover the inner lies that nag at you. Notice those areas in your life in which you're uncomfortable, uneasy, or in a tug-of-war with your inner Self. Notice the areas of your life where you have to admit to yourself that your actions are wrong or not completely honest. Notice when you seem to be defensive. Don't worry about having to be right, or not being wrong. Instead, have the courage to see yourself as honestly as you can.

As you do this, you may feel pain, stress, guilt or insecurity before you begin to experience a lightening up. In the short-term you may not like what you're feeling but keep with it and don't worry. In the long-run, as you sort out lies and half truths from Truth, your path in life will become increasingly easy. In time Truth becomes a constant guide, mapping you through the maze of your mind, emotions and all your real-life problems.

Meditation: Who Am I?

This ancient meditation is one of the best that you can do. By continually contemplating the possible answers to the question, "Who am I?," you'll peel away every limiting concept about yourself to reveal who you really are. With this meditation you travel past the limitations of your mind to discover your true self. You discover the part you carry with you when you die, the ultimate reality that is the same as Love, Truth and Higher Spirit.

The directions for this meditation are very simple, but don't let this apparent simplicity lead you to believe that it's always easy to do. Sometimes it may seem easy (especially at first), and at other times it may be difficult. You may find that your mind rebels, unable to concentrate, defending itself at every turn as you chip away at its defenses and illusions. As you keep doing this meditation, its effects are subtle, far-reaching and powerful, both within your life and within yourself.

The Meditation

1. Sit or lie down with your spine straight, your legs uncrossed, your hands by your sides or on top of your lap with their palms up. Close your eyes.

2. Breathe long, deep breaths in and out of your nose, concentrating on the breath entering and leaving through your nostrils. As you do this, relax and bring your attention entirely to the present.

3. When you feel relaxed and "here," ask and answer this question: "WHO AM I?"

4. Meditate on your answer. Can you imagine yourself
    still existing if you were not that which you answered
    yourself to be? If so, you have not yet found your
    answer. Ask the question again and meditate on the
    answer.

5. Continue to ask yourself "WHO AM I?" until you
    have exhausted every form of self-concept. Ask that
    question until you've exhausted every description or
    feeling you have of yourself. Ask yourself that ques-
    tion, rejecting everything that you are not.

6. You can do this meditation for any time length that
    you like, doing it for a certain period of time every
    day, or "on the run." (If you're somewhere you'll
    attract unwanted attention by closing your eyes, like at
    your office desk, you can do it with your eyes open.)

TRUTH IS

Truth has no limits,
 no endings or beginnings.
It is the heart of the universe,
 and also the glorious center
 of your own radiant soul.

As water, river and ocean
 are of the same essence,
 so are Truth, love and Self.
It is who you are,
 an eternal being in the endless
 present.

Though as formless as wind,
 as spacious as light,
 and as indescribable as love,
 be not fooled.
Truth is of unsurpassed reality.

Truth is quiet and empty,
 yet the more you silently listen,
 the more loudly it's cries resound
 within the cave of your deepest heart.
Surrender yourself to its life-giving voice.

It endlessly reveals itself
    as a constant experience of
    instantaneous and direct knowing.
Dive deeply into it's infinite center
    and find what you have always
    known.

Truth is the path,
    and the compassionate teacher
    who dwells in your heart.
Heed the heart-voice of Truth
    and be opened to the eyes of your
    soul.

Let not the phantoms
    of thought, time and form
    hold your life in their finite hands.
Dear friend, follow Truth's path
    to the source of your own eternity.

CHAPTER SIX

Surrender and Accept

The Fifth Practice

*I*t's impossible to follow this path to the Higher Spirit without learning to surrender. To surrender is to let go of each passing moment, to let it pass, so you can be completely here. It means letting go of all your prejudgments and preconceptions, to find the wisdom of now. It means relinquishing your illusions and mistaken beliefs so that you can begin to experience life as it really is. Only by surrendering can you experience the contentment that results when you accept everything that life brings to you. Only until you let go of what you think your life should be, can you find enjoyment in what it actually is.

> *Surrender the need to "be somebody" and let yourself be "nobody special." Begin to accept yourself as you are, with all your faults and shortcomings, and surrender any false pretenses. Stop trying to be right all the time, and have it be okay to be wrong. When you let down your guard, you'll find yourself becoming much more relaxed. You begin to experience life fully only when you learn to release fear, pride, anger, greed, envy, guilt and shame as they come up for you. When you open your heart to vulnerability, and let go of mistrust, you open yourself to love.*

Be willing to accept anything that comes to you, whether it's a new understanding or a new life circumstance. With that kind of willingness, you may be surprised at the gifts that you receive—including the gift of lasting inner contentment.

It's Not Always Easy to Surrender

It is not always easy to surrender. It can be particularly difficult to do so when you cannot see anything to replace what you're being asked to give up or surrender. You may feel foolish. You may feel frightened or defensive. It's okay to have these feelings. Just notice that they're there and have a little willingness to let go of the attention you're giving them. It can be helpful to say to yourself, "I surrender," and then be willing to be led by the guiding voice of Truth. Don't be disappointed when you find that you have to surrender the same thing over and over again. Rarely do you just surrender once and then it's done.

A True Life Example
of Practical Benefits

It's easy to see how surrendering and accepting can help you emotionally and spiritually. It can also help you in practical ways in the day-to-day events of your life. For example, the ability to surrender my preconceptions and images of myself and accept the truth helped me immensely not so long ago. A few years back, I had just invested everything I had to buy the jewelry business from my ex-husband. Soon after that, my accountant told me that I was losing a tremendous amount of money each month in my crystal jewelry business, and that if I continued on this route, I was going to go bankrupt. As if to reconfirm what I was told, the various banks, creditors and other financial institutions to which I owed money, started calling me. Of course, they were all asking for more money than I had... and they wanted it immediately.

Up to this point, I had left my crystal jewelry business in the hands of various managers, assuming that all I had to do was to continue designing the jewelry, which gave me time to write the crystal book, do the various music and guided meditation cassettes and do workshops. It was all nicely set up—or so I thought until this point. Now all of a sudden I had to let go of my illusory "perfect picture" about what was happening and realize that something was "off kilter." I had to let go of all my feelings about "being successful" and admit to the reality that I might have to go bankrupt. I also had to surrender my idea that a company that was heartful and doing so much good for people couldn't fail. I needed to look at the entire reality of the situation instead of indulging in wishful thinking, running in panic or immediately declaring bankruptcy.

It was only when I could let go of these limiting feelings and preconceptions that I could move forward in a way that was effective and successful. I immediately got involved again in the day-to-day management of the business, trying to pinpoint the problems. I started on the search for experienced business people that could let me know exactly what my business problems were. I also learned as much as I could about business operations and finances, again letting go of any pretense that I "knew that I was doing, so needed no help." As much as possible, I tried to surrender to the personal and business situation that I was in, seeing it realistically instead of misleading myself with all my fears and projections. (This wasn't easy when teams of lawyers and bankers would grill me endlessly over the phone, when I was recovering from a near-death situation and had a new baby!)

I also had to let go of my old sense of who I was in life. My meditation became to continually uproot any clinging that I had to an identity based on any part of the crystal jewelry business or of being a crystal person, a new age person, a healer, a teacher, or any other role that could define my sense of identity apart from who I really was deep down inside. This was a continual process of constantly keeping in view my real Self rather than any other emotions or thoughts that arose that seemed to be based on any other identity. It was only as I did this that I had the room to see the mistakes and the solutions, keep my emotional balance, and make the necessary business changes. Now my company is successful again.

As shown in this example, when you're able to surrender, not only will you be able to advance along a path of self-discovery, but you'll be able to improve your daily life. When you can let go, instead of staying stuck in unprofitable, dangerous, or unhealthy situations, you're able to move on. You'll be able to not only find a solution, but to have the means to do it, whether it entails restructuring a business, declaring bankruptcy, changing jobs or moving from where you live. If you're in an unhealthy relationship, you'll be able to let go and change it. If someone leaves you, or a relationship ends, you'll know that it doesn't mean the end of your life, even though it may feel like it at the time. Fear and insecurity will no longer keep you in life situations that compromise your own integrity or happiness.

The Process of Surrendering

Sometimes it's not immediately obvious what it is we need to surrender. Anytime you feel yourself become angry or defensive, know that there is something underneath that would be valuable to surrender. Sometimes it isn't easy to identify what that is. But the good news is that it's usually not necessary to identify it. We can still surrender. All we need is to *be willing to be willing* to surrender. This begins the process of letting go. After awhile surrendering this way will become second nature. Eventually you can live you entire life in a state of constant surrender.

Surrender doesn't mean that you stop being an active, creative participant in life. You still remain an active life participant. It just means that you give up everything that is in the way of living in the state of Truth. It means that you are no longer driven by fear. It means knowing that you always have within you what it takes to solve all of your life puzzles and challenges. No longer limited by your preconceptions, more solutions are available to you. The more you surrender, the more you erase all limitations.

In order to surrender, you need to be able to trust. Let go, and trust the Higher Spirit. Accept the fact that you can't control life, no matter how hard you try. (In fact, the less you surrender, the more life controls you.) Give up your self-defensive posture and put yourself in the Higher Spirit's hands. Go ahead and trust. This is what Jesus meant when he said "Consider ye the lilies of the field. Neither do they toil nor worry, yet they are robed in more splendor than kings." This is what is written in the Bible, "Though you walk through the valley of the shadow of death, I am with you."

What It Feels Like to Surrender

*O*nce you surrender, you'll feel an immediate relief. It's like step-ping out of a small stuffy box into the open air. You'll feel a spacious-ness within you that you didn't have before. You'll feel a certain lightness inside, like you've just dropped pounds from your body and a heavy weight from your mind. When you've surrendered, there's nothing to try to become, to fight against or defend anymore. You can let down the walls that enclose and protect your heart and just let yourself be. When that happens, you'll feel the love that lies dor-mant in your heart begin to awaken in all its precious vulnerability and joyfulness. Your mind will gently stop racing and your body will slowly start to release its tension. You're finally able to relax—you can let go of your tight jaw, your aching back and shoulders or your clenched stomach. Your breathing will eventually become deeper and slower, your lungs able to freely expand as your mind and emo-tions begin to calm. To surrender is to feel a wonderful inner free-dom, like the blossoming of Spring, or the first breath of dawn.

Affirmations To Help You Surrender

*R*epeating affirmations silently or out loud is one of the best methods that you can use to surrender and accept. Not only is this method extremely effective, but it's appropriate in any life situation. I've constantly repeated this affirmation or prayer for years: "Not my will, but thine." It's effects are powerful and immediate. It constantly reminds me to surrender myself and to trust in the care and guidance of a higher, more lasting reality than my small, individual ego of constantly changing desires and fears. It is an affirmation one is able to employ in virtually any and every challenge life might offer us, from the aggravation of a difficult co-worker to the challenge of a serious illness.

Here are some other affirmations for strength, surrender and acceptance. Try saying them to yourself and see which one feels best to you. Then continue to repeat it to yourself whenever you need to surrender, whenever you're afraid or doubtful, whenever you feel that you need extra strength, or whenever you want to remind yourself to let go. Let the words of these affirmation sink deep within your soul, allowing you to build your trust. Let these words free you from all that imprisons your heart.

Affirmations for Surrender and Trust

1. "I place myself in Your hands."

2. "My heart is Yours."

3. "I give to You my fear."

4. "I surrender to your infinite peace."

5. "All I have is Yours."

6. "Yours is the way of Happiness."

7. "All I am is You."

8. "Not my will but Thine."

9. "I am fine just as I am."

10. "I trust Your voice in my heart."

11. "I offer you my body, heart, mind and soul."

12. "You are my divine shepherd, and I shall not want."

Of course, these aren't the only affirmations that you can use. If none of these work well for you, reach deep into your inner Self and discover one that does. To do this, let yourself relax in an attitude of surrender and see what words reflect how you feel. Hear the words that come from your own heart.

Acceptance

As *was said earlier, acceptance is the natural next* step after surrender. In fact, the two are often intertwined like two branches of the same vine. Where surrender is a feeling of release, acceptance is a feeling of "filling up" or "taking in." Acceptance is deeply life affirming. As with surrender, you can't accept from the past or the future, only from the present. To have an attitude of surrender and acceptance means that you accept everything, even your decisions and actions to change something. You accept the "bad" as well as the "good." You accept those times when you don't do the right thing or what you know you should do. There is nothing you can't accept— even your own non-acceptance.

Often, having this inner sense of acceptance doesn't seem logical. You feel sadness and outrage as you look around in the world, for example, and see people fighting and killing each other. You feel the immense pain of so many people suffering, and it seems so wrong and senseless. It can be difficult to reconcile acceptance in the face of so much wrong. There is another reality, however, in which all the pain and tragedy makes sense. From this perspective, it all has a purpose that is beyond our emotional and rational minds to understand. When observing wars, killings and other forms of suffering from the perspective of this reality, there is no changing it. It's neither right nor wrong. It is simply the way it is. All that you can do is observe and understand. At the same time, there is another reality, (the one we're most familiar with), in which this immense human suffering is wrong.

Acceptance, Desire and Change

I have spent much of my life trying to understand this often paradoxical problem of surrender and acceptance. I had been greatly influenced and moved by the ancient text on enlightenment called *Hsin Hsin Ming*, by Sengstan, the Third Zen Patriarch. The key to this path of awakening is given in the first sentence that begins, "The Great Way is not difficult for those who have no preferences." In trying to apply this in my life, I mistakenly thought that it meant that I should try not to care one way or another about what was happening to me. I reasoned that this meant that there should be no difference to me whether someone loved or hated me, whether someone treated me well or terribly, whether I was doing something I liked or something I didn't. I thought that I shouldn't do anything to try to be either happy or unhappy. Anything I was feeling should be just merely observed, rather than changed, because changing something meant that I had a preference.

I figured that the fastest way to learn this was to either put myself in situations that I didn't like, or let myself be treated in ways that I didn't like, and then try to develop equanimity. So many times, rather than head away from things that evoked strong negative reactions in me, I steered right towards them and tried to remain present centered and retain my equanimity. In that way I thought that I wouldn't feel the need to change anything because I'd have no more preferences.

I also worked with the Buddhist teaching that said that desire (having preferences) was the cause of all suffering. I thought that in order to be enlightened, you were supposed to have no desire. (This is another common spiritual misunderstanding.) So for years, I tried to surrender all my desires. If I found that I had a desire for money, for example, I gave away everything that I had. If I liked my long hair, I cut it off. If I had a desire for sex, I became celibate. If I had a desire for a comfortable house, I gave up my place to live and moved to an ashram or other more humble situation. Even when I had nothing but my sleeping blanket, a few things to wear, and a small altar for meditation, there was still one problem: The faster I seemed to surrender one desire, the faster it was replaced by another. It seemed endless!

Finally, after years of giving things up, trying to understand the nature of my attachment to desire, I realized the truth. My happiness, my state of mind, and my awareness of the Spirit within, didn't have a thing to do with the constant surrendering of my things, my desires or anything else based on those desires. I learned that the "having no preferences" of the *Hsin Hsin Ming* didn't mean what I thought it did. I saw that my inner contentment was based on something much deeper than my desires, which just like any other thought or emotion, just came and went. To surrender my desires or my preferences, didn't mean that I wasn't supposed to try not to have them. Instead, I could remain unattached to them, letting them come and go while remaining centered on who I really was in essence. This is true of "good" desires and well as "bad" desires.

Having no preferences, then, means surrendering the need to have things be one way or another in order to experience the underlying reality. Then you're able to remain perfectly Self-aware no matter what thoughts or feelings you're having and no matter what is happening. You can be yourself no matter what. You could be Self-aware during change, and Self-aware during no-change.

The other thing that the *Hsin Hsin Ming* teaches, is that to accept something doesn't mean that you have to condone it or not change it. Neither acceptance nor surrender are meant to be recipes for action or non-action. Instead, rather than implying that you shouldn't change anything, they offer you a way stop blindly reacting, and instead to see the truth, to see things the way they are. Instead of telling you not to act, they allow you to act more effectively and more consciously. Only with acceptance can you gain the deep understanding of a problem that brings lasting solutions.

Surrender, Acceptance and Happiness

*A*cceptance isn't a prescription for an attitude of "anything goes." All your actions still make a difference. You will still reap what you sow—cause and effect still applies. If you act harshly to another, for example, not only will they act that way towards you, but you'll harden your heart, making it difficult to feel peaceful and loving. If you're dishonest, not only won't others believe you, but you'll also suffer the inner hollowness of abandoning your own integrity. When you're hurting yourself or others, you can't live your life with the balance and insight that it takes to follow the path to self-development.

When you surrender completely, accepting life fully, you'll find that you need less and less to make you happy. Your desires begin to lessen. When you don't need much, it gets easier to have what you do need. You'll find out how little you really need to be happy. In fact, you'll soon discover that you have everything that you really need to be happy, because happiness doesn't depend on things. It's already inside of you and you only need to find it. It is only when you live in this state of acceptance that you can have it all. So don't be afraid. Let down your inner guard. Let down your protective walls and trust that everything will be all right. Trust that you'll be taken care of; live in a state of constant surrender, for that is the key to your own lasting happiness.

Meditation: Surrendering Attachment To Desires

The following meditation will teach you to merely observe the constant coming and going of desire in your mind instead of feeling compelled to seek its satisfaction. When you can just notice your

wants, surrendering the need to act on them, you can find ⟨
deeper needs they are based on. When you uncover the deepe ⸝⸝
you find out what will bring you true contentment. You no longer
have to seek satisfaction of passing desires in order to find your fulfillment. No longer chasing after these transient desires your life becomes far simpler, filling you with a feeling of wholeness. No matter
whether you do this meditation formally or informally, eventually
you'll notice yourself to be less and less at the mercy of your desires.

The Meditation

1. Sit upright or lie on your back with your spine
   straight. Rest your hands, palm up, either in your lap
   or down beside you. With your legs uncrossed and
   face forward, let your eyes close.

2. Take three long, deep breaths in and out through your
   nose, relaxing on each out-breath. Say to yourself,
   "Thy will be mine," or "I surrender," If either of those
   are hard for you to say, just say the word "surrender."

3. Begin to breathe normally, retaining your attention on
   your breath and saying the words "Thy will be done,"
   "I surrender," or "surrender" to yourself. Do this for a
   minute or two, until you are relaxed and present-
   centered.

4. Now shift your attention to your thoughts, asking
    yourself this question, "What do I want?" Start asking
    yourself this question, noticing what answers come up
    for you. Don't think about it, just answer with the first
    words or images that come up for you.

5. As soon as you have identified something that you
    want, hold that thought or image in your mind and
    notice how you feel. How does the thought of having
    or not having this thing that you want you want affect
    the way you feel? When you think about having what
    you're desiring, how do you feel? When you think
    about not having that which you're desiring, how do
    you feel?

6. Focus on these feeling inside of you. Do they arise in
    your heart? Are you not really desiring that which
    is unfulfilled in your own heart?

7. Focus on your heart. Breathe two or three breaths long
    breaths as if they go in and out of your heart. As you
    do this let your chest feel soft. Let go in the middle of
    your back between your shoulder blades. Let go of the
    holding in your stomach and in the small of your back.

Relax the small of your back and let your stomach grow soft as a baby's belly.

8. Now let go. Surrender. Surrender yourself to these feelings inside of your heart. Let yourself have them. Accept yourself—even these feelings. Let go, give up. Give up your resistance. Give up your fighting, your fears, your doubt and your pain. Feel what you feel. Be who you are.

9. Now, begin to feel as if a deep peace is beginning to steal through you. It enters through your heart, filling it to overflow through the rest of your body. As it does, you begin to feel perfectly accepting. Everything's all right. Let go into that inner feeling of trust that fills you with such peaceful contentment. Let that feeling steal through you, body, mind and emotion. Let your inner soul be at rest.

10. Retain this feeling of peaceful fulfillment within you, and envision that a soft, pink light gently begins to flow outward from your heart, through your body, to gradually surround you in an orb of nurturing protection and comfort. The more that you bask in the glow of this pink light, the more soft yet powerful you

feel—the power of infinite peace. If you like, you can say to yourself, "I am filled with a soft pink light which surrounds me in a nurturing orb."

11.   Holding this feeling within you, think again about what it was that you desired. Can you feel, envision, or otherwise experience the desire as existing apart from the inner peace that you feel? Can you retain this feeling of inner peace, and not have the thing it is that you are desiring? Surrender. Let go of that desire. Let it pass from your mind, all the while retaining the feeling of inner peace within you.

12.   Continue to keep the feeling of contentment within you. Rather then grasp it, let go, and let it float cloud-like within your heart. Continue to relax any tightness you feel any place in your body, especially in your lower or middle back. Continue to let go of your belly and soften the middle of your chest. Let your heart feel open.

13.   If another desire comes to your attention, observe it in the same way that you did the last one. Notice how you feel with it's satisfaction or dissatisfaction. Notice the true source of your feelings, then let go of the

desire. Continue this process of surrendering or letting go of your desires as they come up.

14. As you continue this process, it will become easier and quicker. After awhile, you'll no longer have to consciously try to surrender desires. It will seem that their arising is as automatic as their surrendering. You will eventually be able to observe desires appear and disappear like moving clouds across the clear sky of your mind, as your state of inner contentment remains unaffected. You will be in a state of constant surrender and acceptance.

15. When you are through meditating, shift your attention back to your breathing. Take three, long, powerful, deep breaths as if they come from in and out of your heart center in the middle of your chest. Inhale completely, and then exhale forcefully from your heart center. Feel the surface beneath you, recall the environment around you, then open your eyes. As you arise, retain your body's relaxation and your feeling of contentment.

This meditation can be done as a formal sitting for any length of time that you choose. If you don't know how long you should do it, first try it for three minutes. Then, if you like, do it for ten minutes, twenty minutes, a half hour or an hour. To do this meditation "on the run," rather than searching for desires, just let them arise naturally. Then when you notice yourself being attracted to a particularly strong desire (or set of desires), take a few moments to observe and develop non-attachment as in the above exercise.

Besides helping you to transcend desires to discover more lasting happiness, this meditation will help to calm your anxiety, decrease your fears, slow your mind, relax your body, and open your heart to love.

*There Is A Deeper Essence
Contained In Frailty
That Is Misses When One Insists
On Maintaining A
Superior Stance.*

*Surrender False Pride.
It Hides You From The Truth.*

CHAPTER SEVEN

Meditate

The Sixth Practice

*M*editate regularly! Every spiritual
tradition, ancient or modern, gives this
*instruction, whether they use the word
"meditation" or not.*

Meditation is normally thought of as a continual, deep concentration upon a single focus. This focus can be on an object, thought, emotion or experience of something that's in some way special or sacred. This is, however, only part of meditation. With practice, however, you soon discover that meditation is actually something deeper than thought or concentration. Anything that you're doing can be considered meditation because meditation isn't concerned with *what* you do, but only with *how* you do it. If any activity is done

in a manner and purpose to bring you closer to the Spirit, it's meditation. If it takes you further away, it's not. Thus, if your sitting,
praying, or playing with the kids is done in a manner intended to be
meditative, then this action becomes your meditation.

Meditation involves your whole being with the intention that
your activity will lead you to awakening. It involves giving up everything that takes you away from your "beingness" here in the moment. To meditate is to *be*.

Paradoxically, meditation is something that you both do and
don't do. You don't do anything because you merely have to "be" in
order to know reality. On the other hand, in order to learn how to
"be," you have to do something. You can do the six practices that are
outlined in this book in order to learn "not-doing." To observe, to
remember, to follow truth, to be present-centered and to surrender,
form a single meditation that will lead you to a state of beingness
that is beyond all "doingness." When you enter that state of constant beingness, you live in a state of meditation without even trying.
If this isn't clear right now, don't worry. As you practice meditation
everything I've said thus far becomes self-evident.

The Effects of
Meditation

*A*s you meditate, you'll experience both obvious and subtle effects.
Meditation will assist you in letting go of your fears. You'll find
yourself being more relaxed, trusting more, and more able to forgive

and accept. If you make meditation a daily part of your life, you will discover the real meaning of self-knowledge. Even though your life may be difficult you'll find yourself relating to it as a true gift. There's an ancient Native American practice that helps you to experience this kind of gratefulness. First you recall a difficult time or a terrible thing that happened in your life. Then you thank the Great Spirit, recalling the lessons that you, even now, continue to learn from it.

When I first started meditating I soon found I was spending less time feeling afraid and insecure. (I used to be very shy.) I was better able to see what was important in my life and then develop the abilities to focus more attention on those things instead of those less important. This didn't happen all at once. I began to change bit by bit, year after year, as I applied what I learned from meditation. Sometimes it seemed as though I wasn't changing at all, or that I was changing much too slowly. As long as I kept meditating, however, I felt my life improving. Sometimes it seemed much too difficult, other times the reverse was true. Life became a whirlwind of change and excitement. I remember asking a teacher why sometimes I felt ecstatic and other times I felt unhappy. I thought that I should be feeling calm and happy all of the time. He reminded me that no matter what happened, it was okay; I should try not to expect anything one way or another. Especially, I was told not to expect to be happy all of the time just because I was meditating. Whenever I got discouraged because I wasn't happy or because I got upset for some reason, my teacher assured me that this was okay. The important thing was to not pretend that life was different than it actually is; the pretending would slow my progress.

Let Your Whole Life Be Meditation

If you do the six practices in this book your whole life can be a meditation no matter what you're doing, thinking or experiencing.

Meditate and be unafraid of your life. Dive into it wholeheartedly and welcome everything that comes to you as just more fuel for your meditation. Be creative, for there isn't any right or wrong way to do it. However, remember that even though your understanding and self-awareness constantly deepens as you meditate, there's no ending point, or place where you'll "know everything." (As many spiritual teachers like to point out, when you think you "know everything," you're actually showing your ignorance.)

There are many ways to meditate "on the run." When you walk along the street, for example, breathe in the air and feel the cleansing, healing "breath of the Higher Spirit" wash through you with each breath. As other people pass you, see them as fellow spirits, their hearts linked with yours in the reality of the endless present. As you see parents and children, let yourself feel the love and care given to you as a "child of the spirit." Be thankful and regard everything in your life as unfolding to teach you of true reality.

Consistency Is Important

Consistency is important in any meditation, whether done as a formal sitting, or in conjunction with life events. Do any meditation you choose for at least thirty days. Though you'll probably experience some results right away, the deeper effects usually won't come until the end of the thirty day period. This is because meditation builds on itself, each time reaching deeper into your sub-conscious to dissolve even more of the barriers that divide illusion and reality.

Meditation is like doing a jigsaw puzzle. Each time that you do the meditation you add a new puzzle piece. At first, you can't see the picture at all and can only admire some of the colors or patterns that seem to be taking shape. As you keep meditating, you continually add more puzzle pieces, each time seeing more of the picture. Finally, when the last piece is added, you can see the picture as a whole. If you stop too early, you'll never see the complete picture.

It's easy to let your practice slide once your meditation starts working. However, given the fleeting nature of happiness, you'll once again begin to encounter some after some form of pain, loss or unhappiness. When that happens, you'll remember to meditate again.

It's like the story of the man who's lost in a snowstorm. Unable to find his way, he starts desperately praying, "God save me! If you get me out of this I'll give you everything! My whole life will be yours!" As he says this, he spies a distant farmhouse. "Oh God," he prays, "Thank you, thank you! I'll put fifty percent of all my money in the collection plate at church. I'll give more to charity!" Finally, he reaches the door of the farmhouse, pushes it open and the farmer welcomes him in to enjoy a warm fire, dry clothes and food. "Lord," he silently prays, "This is so wonderful, thank you, thank you!" After he has eaten, he is so full that he forgets his promises entirely.

Don't fall into this trap. Instead, give yourself a chance to know the deeper happiness that is so much more real and lasts so much longer than any temporary pleasure. Regard your desire to meditate in the first place as a precious gift given to you by your own inner spirit. Treasure and cultivate this gift. To avoid getting caught in the trap of forgetfulness, start remembering the Higher Spirit at all times. Let your remembrance become as automatic as your own breathing. This remembrance will not only constantly lead you back to your meditation, but will become its cornerstone.

A Meditation Guideline

In the remaining pages of this chapter, I've described six meditation practices. Within these six, you'll also find many different types of meditations as well as suggestions for creating your own practice from the normal activities of your daily life. The instructions I've given includes monthly meditations to be followed in the sequence suggested. The first week in the month, do the meditation for ten minutes a day. The second week, do the meditation for fifteen minutes a day. The third week, do the meditation for twenty minutes a day and the fourth week do it for thirty minutes a day or more.

Along with the monthly meditation you'll find a short sentence describing a "focus" for the day. The idea here is to give your attention to that idea or principle by contemplating it, letting it be an affirmation or by praying about it. As you meditate, let the focus become a deep expression of your own soul.

While meditating, relax and let go of your past and your future, and instead bring your attention steadily into the present. Let go of your doubts and fears. Let the truth within your soul lead you to the experience of complete inner contentment and to the light of your true Self.

Monthly Meditations

MONTH #1

> Meditation: Long Deep Breathing to Become Present-Centered (See Chapter 2.)
> Focus: Dedicate your life to Truth, or the Higher Spirit.

MONTH #2

> Meditation: Observing Your Thoughts (See Chapter 3.)
>
> Focus: Offer your mind to Truth or the Higher Spirit.

MONTH #3

> Meditation: RAMA Meditation (See Chapter 4.)
>
> Focus: Offer your heart to Truth or Higher Spirit.

MONTH #4

Meditation: Meditation on the Self—Who Am I?
(See Chapter 5.)

Focus: Week 1 - Surrender your doubts and fears.

Week 2 - Surrender your anger.

Weeks 3 & 4 - Surrender yourself to Truth.

MONTH #5

Meditation: Surrendering Attachment to Desire (See
Chapter 6.)

Focus: Be no one special, nothing more than yourself
and nothing less than yourself. Be just yourself.

MONTH #6

Meditation: Developing Love, Compassion &
Empathy for Yourself (See Chapter 8.)

Focus: Experience yourself as one with the Higher
Spirit. (If you like, use the affirmation, "Spirit and I
are One.")

MONTH #7

Meditation: Developing Love Compassion &
Empathy for Others (See Chapter 8.)

Focus: Experience yourself as one with others.

MONTH #8

Meditation: OM Meditation (this chapter)

Focus: Experience yourself as being beyond formand description. (If you like, use the affirmation, "I am beyond my body, mind and emotions.")

MONTH #9

Meditation: Navel Point Meditation (this chapter)

Focus: Dedicate your growing strength to the Higher Spirit or Truth. (If you like, use the affirmation, "My source of my strength lies within my heart.")

MONTH #10

Meditation: OM Meditation (this chapter)

Focus: Dedicate your soul to Truth or Higher Spirit.

MONTH #11

Meditation: Meditation on the Self: Who Am I? (See Chapter 5.)

Focus: Dedicate yourself to service in the world, or helping others.

MONTH #12

Meditation: RAMA Meditation (See Chapter 4.)

Focus: Offer your heart to the Higher Spirit.

NOTE: When you have completed this sequence, you may repeat it over again each year indefinitely. As an alternative, once you have done this year, you may elect to do, instead, one of the meditations from month #1, #2, #3, #4 or #8 as a regular practice.

Om Meditation

This meditation will activate your "third eye," the subtle energy center of intuition, creativity and wisdom, located near the center of your forehead. It can also activate the crown center, located roughly on or over the top of your head. To activate this center will bring you "cosmic consciousness" (for lack of a better word), or spiritual wisdom. As we said in Chapter 4, *Om* is said to be the primal sound of the universe, the sound associated with the place of all beginnings and endings, the sound underlying all manifestation.

The Meditation

1. Sit or lie down with your spine straight, your legs uncrossed, and your hands resting palm-up in your lap or by your sides. Close your eyes.

2. Take a few moments to breathe with long, deep gentle breaths through your nose, completely filling and

emptying your lungs without straining for breath. As
you do this, focus on your breath entering and leaving
your body. Continue this until you feel relaxed,
centered and focused.

3. Shift your focus to your "third eye" center in the
    middle of your forehead, and the crown center in the
    middle of the top of your head. As you do this, begin
    to breathe normally. Feel as if your breath is entering
    through the center of your forehead and leaving,
    upward, through the top center of your head.

4. Say the word *OM*, (pronounced ohm), silently to
    yourself on every in-breath and out-breath. Continue
    to feel as if your breath enters through the center of
    your forehead and leaves through the top of your head
    while you say the word *OM*.

5. Continually let go of any tension or strain that comes
    to your attention, feeling it leave your body on every
    out-breath.

6. If you become aware of any other intruding thoughts,
    feelings or any other distraction, release your attention

from it, bringing it back to the silent sound of *OM*
and your breath which enters your forehead and leaves
through the top of your head.

7. At the finish of the meditation, take three long, deep
    breaths through your nose, releasing them forcefully
    through your mouth as you bring your attention back
    to yourself and your surroundings. Open your eyes and
    stretch your body.

Meditation for Strength Of Will, Endurance And Vitality

The navel center (described in step 3, below), also known as the
seat of the will, is the center associated with strength, endurance
"will power" and vitality. It gives you both the subtle and physical
nervous strength to remain calm under stress, to handle any
difficulty, and to keep on going when it seems impossible. When
this center is strengthened and stimulated, it gives you strength of
purpose and a sense of physical well-being. It will help keep you
healthy. Whenever you feel tired and need a lift, this is an excellent
meditation to do. It gives you the ability to manifest the realizations
of your heart, intuition and spirit into "real-life" reality. Not only
that, it will help you to maintain a sense of balance and as you open
yourself to new subtle and spiritual realities.

The Meditation

1. Sit or lie down with your spine straight, your legs uncrossed and your hands on your lap or down by your side, palms up.

2. Close your eyes and breathe naturally. Let yourself feel more and more peaceful and relaxed with every out-breath.

3. Focus on your navel center which lies approximately two inches below your belly button and about two inches inward. Begin to feel as if your breath is flowing in and out of this point. Continue to breathe in and out of your navel center like this for about three minutes.

4. Now, visualize a bright yellow light flowing into your navel center with every in-breath. With every out-breath, it begins to fill your belly with a the warm, golden glow of a gently swirling fire. As you continue to pull in this yellow light with every in-breath, feel with every out-breath as if this warm glowing fire slowly fills your entire body. Feel as if you're expanding, getting stronger with every breath. Feel as if you're filled with the shining vitality of the sun, radiating a powerful, yet gentle, warmth and sense of glorious well-being.

5. See in your mind's eye the yellow glowing light
    expands beyond your body to surround you in an egg-
    shaped orb in which you feel powerfully expanded.

6. After you have surrounded yourself in this glowing
    egg-shaped orb of light, bring your attention back to
    your navel center. Silently say the sounds HA (hah), as
    your breath enters your navel center, and RA (rah), as
    your breath leaves your navel center. Do this for at
    least three minutes.

7. Now bring your attention to your heart center in the
    middle of your chest. Feel as if the warm vital, glow
    within you now radiates from the vicinity of your heart
    center. Begin to breathe as if your breath enters and
    leaves through your heart center. Silently say the
    sounds RA as your breath enters, and MA as it leaves.
    Feel your heart relax and open, sending love and inner
    peace throughout your entire body and mind.

8. When you feel filled with love, breathe normally, open
    your eyes and stretch your body, retaining the warm,
    golden glow of vitality and strength both within and
    without.

Salute to the Sun

The following is a series of simple positions or yoga poses that can be done to support all of the meditations in the book, whether you're doing the prior monthly series of meditations along with the six practices, or just the six practices themselves. This yoga series will keep your body healthy, and your mind and emotions calm, as well as attuning and aligning you to the inner reality of your own heart. Because of this, it is excellent to do as a daily practice or as often as you like. If you can't do all the poses perfectly, do as best as you're able. Don't worry, you'll continually do it better as your body becomes more flexible. The important thing to remember is to relax into each pose rather than forcing yourself into it. Hold the pose as gently as possible for anywhere from a few moments to several minutes. Hold each pose for an equal length of time.

The Poses

1. SALUTATION POSE.

Stand upright with your feet
together. Place your palms
flat together and hold them
in front of your heart. Point
your fingers upward.

2. UPWARD SALUTATION POSE.

Still standing upright with
your feet together, stretch
your arms up over your head
and gently bend backwards
as far as you can.

3. HANDS-TO-FEET POSE.

Bend forward and place
your hands on the floor or
ground beside your feet.
Keeping your legs straight,
bring your forehead towards
your knees.

4. ONE-FOOT-EXTENDED POSE.

Keeping your palms flat on
the floor, stretch your left
leg straight back, resting the
knee on the floor. Bend your
right knee in front of your
chest. Now look upward.

5. BOTH-FEET-EXTENDED POSE.

Stretch your right leg back
alongside your left leg so
that only your hands and
feet touch the floor. Your
head, back and legs should
form a straight line.

6. EIGHT-LIMBS-BOWING POSE.

Lower your body and touch
your forehead, chest, knees
and feet to the floor or
ground. With your elbows
up, rest your palms on the
floor beside your chest.

7. SNAKE POSE.

With your toes and knees still
touching the floor or ground,
raise your head and chest up by
straightening your arms. As you
keep your shoulders raised, bend
your head back and look up.

8. MOUNTAIN POSE.

Keeping your arms and legs
straight, and your head down,
raise your buttocks. Try to touch
your heels to the floor. Your
body should look like a mountain or an upside-down "V."

9. ONE-FOOT-EXTENDED POSE.

Bring your left foot forward
between your hands. Keep
your right leg stretched
backwards with your right
knee and toes touching the
floor or ground. Look up.
(This is the same pose as #4,
with the legs reversed.)

10. HANDS-TO-FEET POSE.

Bring your right foot up to meet
the left. Keeping your legs
straight, bring your forehead
towards your knees. Try touching
your palms to the floor or ground.
(This pose is the same one as #3.)

11. UPWARD SALUTATION POSE.

Standing upright, raise your
arms up over your head and
gently bend backwards as far
as you can. (This is the same
pose as #2.)

12. SALUTATION POSE.

Lower your arms and place
your palms together in front
of your heart center. (This
brings you back to pose #1
where you started.)

When you finish this series of poses, take a few moments to notice how differently you feel. Move gently at first so that you can maintain this new state of consciousness for as long as possible as you begin to go about your day.

The Importance of a Spiritual Family

While all the material in this book can help you live a more meditative life, it can be very beneficial to be around others who are meditating. You'll be able to share experiences, and lend and receive support and comfort when it's needed. It's much easier to face difficulties when you know that others have already dealt with them. Even though others give you advice or feedback, however, continue to follow your own inner guidance.

Where can you find others who are meditating? Go to your local New Age book store or center and ask there. Look for bulletin board notices in your library or community center. Look in the yellow pages and see what's listed under "meditation" or "yoga." Or, start your own group of people who meditate together once a week or once a month. If you find that you need inspiration or instruction, spiritual books, videos, cassettes or other such materials can help. Recorded guided meditations are excellent for both instruction and inspiration.

Finally, when you lead a life of meditation, know that you're part of a special family, each joined in the eternal Spirit that is slowly revealing itself within our hearts. As you bring awakening and new joy to your own life, so too, do you help awaken and uplift the world around you.

BE STILL

When you don't know what to do,
    Be still.

When you don't know what to say,
    Be quiet.

When you rush around
    Like a dog after its own tail,

And clutter the clear sky
    With empty words,

How can you possibly hear
    The longed-for answers

That echo their clear certainty
    Inside your heart.

WITH PROPER ATTENTION,
ALL LIFE IS MEDITATION.

CHAPTER EIGHT

Progression on the Path

E *ven though each person has their own particular path, there are many things that happen and new changes that are common to all. Here are a few of the more usual: As you begin to do these practices you will eventually feel more relaxed. Your thoughts and emotions will no longer seem quite so compelling. Your breathing will become slower and deeper. You will feel anxiety, fear and doubt lessen their hold on you. As you begin to be more identified with something deeper in yourself, you'll feel healthier and more full of life. It's not unusual to have health problems clear up. Eventually you begin to feel lighter,*

as if part of the load you're carrying has been
lifted, even if your responsibilities are the same.

When these things begin to happen, it's not unusual to feel euphoric. You feel as if everything is perfect, as if you somehow possess the key to life. When you first start opening to what is deeper inside you, you often feel as if you're filled with pure life force, or golden light. When you look outward, it's easy to just see the projection of this sense of inner perfection. As time goes by, however, the euphoria passes. Perhaps your meditation practices become more difficult. As you continue to observe yourself, old wounds may resurface, providing you with an opportunity to heal them, or something happens in your life to set your mind racing again. Or possibly nothing so dramatic happens. The euphoria just begins to fade.

When this initial euphoria passes, life can feel dull by comparison. The usual reaction at this point is to try to hold on to the "high" because regular life just doesn't seem like enough for you. All the time, if you look deeply within yourself, you wonder where the euphoria went, or if it was real in the first place. You may feel a little silly as if you somehow aren't worthy or you didn't do something right. In classical spiritual literature, this is known as "the dark night of the soul."

Don't worry. It is natural for the euphoria to come and go many times. When you feel euphoric or "high," enjoy it, and know that it will pass. Don't try to be "high" all the time. To cling to the state of euphoria is to stop your progress. Let it pass. Being awakened is not about being "high," but about discovering something much more enduring.

Love and Vulnerability

After practicing awhile, you find that you're much more able to let down your guard and drop your defenses than ever before. When you do that, the walls around your heart that you've constructed to protect you from hurt begin to crumble. Your heart begins to open. You begin to soften inside, feel what others are feeling. You become flooded with compassion and love for all people and living beings, experiencing everyone and everything as being interrelated. This love is not romance or "falling in love," but something different, a love without conditions or boundaries   because we experience our spiritual connection with everyone, beyond the individual ego. We are able to relate at a "soul" level rather than just a personality level, so our love doesn't depend on what the other person does or says. It is just there, shining as a warm glow within. When you're able to ex- perience love like this, you realize that this love is always there whether you are closed or open to it. The more that you open to it, the more you feel its soft, quiet ecstasy.

To know this love is not all ecstasy, however. To have empathy is to feel others' pain as well as their happiness. To be open is to feel your own pain. There can seem to be so much suffering in the world that every effort to help can seem insignificant. You may find yourself questioning your right to be happy when others are suffering. However, as you progress further, you will learn that you are not powerless to help. You don't have to do "big" things to help. A kind word to someone who is lonely, a helping hand for a hurt child is important too. Be open to love and happiness and find your own way to help. You will be guided by the love and wisdom that is within you.

When your heart first opens, you often feel vulnerable and sensitive. At first you may not know how to be comfortable about your own vulnerability. In time, this discomfort will pass as you get in touch with that part of us all that can never be hurt, that part which underlies even the worst pain.

When you are your most empathetic it's not unusual to become the classic "doormat." You'll do almost anything so that others aren't hurt. You'll sacrifice yourself to the pain, rather than see others suffer. Such self-sacrifice is usually not as loving as it seems. You're not really causing less pain when you sacrifice yourself to avoid the wounding. Underneath it all you may feel hurt, angry and resentful, stuffing down any feelings that might be upsetting—because it seems to be the more loving thing to do.

If you're doing this, you eventually begin to feel terrible inside, the stuffed feelings eating away at you. You may get sick, confused, tense or depressed. You may cover these feelings with a veneer of humility. And then, in spite of your best intentions, your heart begins to close . You're back where you started, somewhat the worse for wear.

It's helpful to remember that you're not that fragile, nor are others. It's not necessarily a terrible thing to feel pain. When you stop resisting your hurt you discover that feeling hurt gives you the chance to experience your vulnerability—and this can be the doorway to self-awareness. When you feel pain, instead of holding back, take a deep breath and relax. Then say or do the honest thing. Don't be afraid to assert yourself. Real love thrives on real communication and dies with dishonesty. Not only that, but practically speaking, everything that you do will be more effective with honesty and true communication.

Getting angry and hurt doesn't mean that you aren't also loving, because the love inside of you exists much deeper than your temporary feelings and thoughts. Love is unchanging and everything else merely passes over its surface. So, open your heart and acknowledge what you are really experiencing. Be angry if you are. Be hurt if you are. To let yourself feel these feelings doesn't make you a bad person, it makes you a real person. Go ahead and protect your personal boundaries. You can do so without closing your heart. Don't let people take advantage of you. Eventually you will find that love is stronger than you think and that people actually appreciate your honesty far more than your fear and false protectiveness.

Open Heart, Closed Heart

*I*t is *likely that your heart will close and open over* and over again. When it closes, it feels as if you're pulled into yourself, as if you've contracted, from what was fluid and soft into what is now hard and solid. No longer do you feel loving and expansive. You feel protective of yourself, again erecting barriers. You may start feeling defensive, antagonistic or fearful. Sometimes these signs are obvious, at other times subtle. After experiencing even a slight opening of your heart, it can be painful to find it closed again. However, don't try to force your heart to feel other than it does. Don't pretend to be loving. If you do that, you and everyone else will feel your deceit. You're not a "bad" or inferior person if you find your heart closed. Be gentle and forgiving of yourself. In the process, you will learn to be gentle and forgiving of others, even while maintaining your personal boundaries. Your entire environment will reflect this heartfulness, nurturing you and everyone with whom you have contact.

When you feel your heart closed, and want to open it, do the six practices and focus on what is deeper within you than the ups and downs of passing emotions. Then your heart will soon open again. Eventually, after this happens a few times, you'll have a faster "recovery time." Each time that your heart opens you will realize the love never left you. Instead, it was patiently waiting within for you to find it again.

Each time you feel unhappy feeling you'll also feel an even deeper, more substantial reality beneath it. Though simple and quiet, this underlying love will be far more present and immediate to you than any of your temporary feelings. The unhappy feelings will not seem so important to you and will tend to leave you quickly. You probably won't feel "in love" all the time. Instead you will find yourself becoming increasingly more happy. Negative feelings will be like passing mirages, certainly not important enough to pay much attention to.

The Third Eye

When traveling this path of self-discovery, your mind will become steady and calm. You'll be able to concentrate without being pulled "off-course" by intruding thoughts. Gradually, as you learn to listen to the guiding voice within, you'll become extremely intuitive. As you use your intuition, you may eventually develop a sixth sense that in some ways is far more sensitive and accurate than your eyes, ears, and other physical senses. This sixth sense is like intuition, yet it is far more developed than that. (The Eastern spiritual traditions call it seeing with the third eye.) With the development of this "sixth sense" some people become aware of deeper realities beyond what appears to our physical senses. They can "hear" what others are thinking even when they don't talk. Dreams become so vivid that they seem no different than "real life." They even learn to enter their own dreams, consciously directing and acting in them. With the development of this "sixth sense" some people become psychic, clairvoyant or clairaudient, able to "see" energetically, becoming aware of auras and subtle energy flows in other people or the environment. They may develop the ability to heal with their hands, eyes or even their intention. They may travel in the astral and other realms, or communicate with animals, plants or stones. They may become aware of non-physical beings, such as angels, spiritual teachers or different earth spirits, and be able to communicate with them.

It is possible, of course, to become so entranced with these awakened abilities don't want to do anything else. Don't get carried away with them. It is important to keep in mind that true mastery consists in the ability to remain functioning and balanced in the everyday world as well as other realities. Shift your focus into your heart for this balance. If you are speaking about your experiences, do it in a way that you can be understood or that is relevant to other's life experience. Or don't say anything at all.

If you begin to experience any other the abilities associated with this "sixth sense," keep your focus on the true, enduring reality within. This will help you to avoid getting carried away with a false sense of your own importance. Treat these awakened abilities merely as signposts that you have progressed along the path rather than signs that you're better than other people. It can be tempting to look down at others from imagined heights, seduced by power and pride. If you succumb to the seduction, however, know that you are setting yourself up for a fall. When you focus on the powers instead of the source of these powers, they will leave you and you will have again lost your Self. For this reason many spiritual traditions instruct you not to use any of these special abilities at all, recommending instead, that you just notice them and continue your practice.

Keep Practicing

*A*s *you continue your practice you may, at times,* reach a plateau in which it seems you're not progressing. This may be frustrating. Or you may decide that you can go no further. You may have decided that you are enjoying yourself with this degree of enlightenment and therefore have no interest in going forward. But the fact is that change is occurring, even though it doesn't seem so. There are many subtle changes happening within you at this point. As long as you are doing the practices, you are progressing. even if you are not aware of it. You will reach many plateaus during the course of your practice. Many times it may seem as if you're going backwards. No matter what you experience, keep on practicing. Persevere. If you do, you will eventually experience the results you desire.

Opening the Heart
(Practices That Can Be Done
in Daily Life)

Following are things you can do to help your heart open more quickly, and to open it again when you find it closed. As with the other meditations, exercises and visualizations in this book, you can do this as a regular practice for a set amount of time every day, as well as anytime during your daily life.

Meditation to Develop Love, Compassion, Acceptance and Empathy for Yourself

The injunction "love thy neighbor as thyself " doesn't only mean to love others, but also to love yourself. If you can't love yourself, you can't begin to love another. If you can't love another, you can't love the Higher Spirit. To help develop love for yourself, you can do this meditation. You can do this for as much or little time as you like.

1.   Stand in front of a mirror, close your eyes, calm and center yourself.

2.   When you feel centered, open your eyes and gaze at your image in the mirror. Look deeply into your own eyes as you see them in the mirror.

3.   As you look into your own eyes, what do you feel? What judgments do you notice that you have? What do you like? What do you dislike? Notice every thought and feeling that arises.

4.   As each thought or feeling arises, release your attachment to it, imagining it floating gently into the ground beneath you where it slowly disappears. You

can imagine the thought or feeling enclosed in a
bubble of water, sinking slowly down to the ground
and then being soaked up by the earth.

5. Next, while you continue gazing into your eyes (in the
   mirror), begin to let your heart open by relaxing the
   center of your chest and imagining that your heart
   opens like the petals of a flower. As you sense yourself
   softening, let the feelings of compassion and love grow
   within your heart.

6. Send these feelings of compassion, acceptance and
   love to your image in the mirror. As you do that,
   continue to soften and open your heart, taking in
   these feelings. Maintain this feeling of love even when
   you finish this meditation and go about the day.

Meditation to Develop Love, Acceptance, Compassion and Empathy for Others

This practice can be done anytime, any place and with another person. The other person doesn't need to do this with you for it to work, so you can even choose a person that you don't know who just happens to be in your vicinity. It's especially useful to do when you find that your heart has closed to a person with whom you're inter-acting. Do this if you're feeling threatened, hurt, angry, or just not "connected" with another.

1. Relax and center yourself as you focus your attention toward the person that you have selected.

2. As you continue to look at this other person, also become aware of yourself. Let the middle of your chest soften and your heart open. Let a feeling of compassion and complete self acceptance grow within your heart. If you find that you can't relax into this loving self-acceptance, then accept this. It's okay that there are parts of yourself you don't like. Continue to feel love for yourself anyway.

3. Next, send this acceptance and love out to the other
    person. Imagine it as a soft stream of light that flows
    from your heart into the other's heart. Surround them
    with love.

4. If you notice thoughts arising that cause you to resist
    sending them love, note them and let them go. As you
    do this, soften the middle of your chest, open your
    heart again, and send them even more love, especially
    to that part of them that you find yourself resisting.

5. As you send the other love, also remain aware of
    yourself. Now, feel them to be the same as you are
    inside their hearts. If you find this hard to do, just
    pretend that they are the same as you inside; then you
    will find that your resistance fades. Feel as if you are
    the same person, as if you share the same beingness
    inside. All the while, continue to open your heart to
    the love inside.

It's great to do this meditation with your children, lover, friend
or spouse, because it is even more powerful when two (or more)
people do it together. Your relationship will deepen and become
more nurturing and fulfilling. When two of you are doing this
meditation together, both of you send this love out to the other, and

feel the other as yourself. At the same time, both of you allow yourselves to feel the love the other person is sending. When you find that you're not communicating in your relationship, or that your heart is closed, do this exercise.

When your heart center is closed, not only do you feel less love, but you suffer physical ramifications that may even effect your health. You start to constrict the area in the middle of your chest. Your chest falls and your shoulders tend to round forward. At the same time, you tend to develop back pain in the area between your shoulder blades. It's as if you're folding in on yourself. Then, in order to compensate for your rounded shoulders and constricted chest, you need to raise your chin in order to hold your head straight. When you do this, you constrict (or close) the energy center in your throat and cut off the subtle energy flow upward into your head. This may result in sore throats, headaches, weakened stomach muscles and/or lower back pain. You may also have a tendency towards indigestion.

To help your heart open, then, it is useful to do exercises to stretch and open your chest. Any form of bending backwards is good. (It's not necessary to do a full backbend.) You can clasp your hands behind your back and, while still clasped, raise them upward towards your head. If you do yoga, the camel pose can be very helpful. A very subtle, yet still effective stretch is to stand upright, feeling tall and straight, and holding your chin level. Extend both arms outward to your side with your hands open and fingers outstretched. While holding this position, feel as if your arms are being gently pulled outward as you keep relaxing your chest. If you like, you can imagine invisible streamers of light flowing outward from your chest, down your arms and out from the tips of your fingers. Anytime that you're outdoors in the sun, you can imagine that you inhale sunlight into your heart center in the middle of your chest. As you breathe this sunlight into your heart center, imagine your chest expanding and your heart opening with the warmth of love.

As an alternative, if you're outside in fresh clean air, you can imagine that with every in-breath you pull this wonderful air into the center of your chest. At the same time that you do this, feel as if the fresh air is clearing your heart of all sorrow, all anger, all wounds, opening in clarity and light. Use your breath, feeling your heart opening on every in-breath, and relaxing on every out-breath.

All of the visualizations and meditations in this book which use the sound "AH" or RAMA are excellent for opening your heart. Finally, listen to heartful music or have it playing as ambient background in your environment. I have recorded *Watergarden* for just this purpose. Relax and let its softly interweaving tones, peaceful pulse and angelic melodies fill your soul with deep peace. Rare is the heart which can resist joyful, peaceful, or inspiring tone, melody or song.

THE GREAT MYSTERY

Though the soul-sun
shines so brightly
in the core of our love,
why do we sometimes linger
in the shadows of darkness?

What unknown voice
of invisible meaning
beckons so enticingly
from the black night
of light's edge?

Great Mystery,
it is you who calls.
Sing to our eager souls
your infinite songs
of endless becomings.
Spirit Voice of siren song,
Sing your poignant stillness,
and let us embrace
your dark depths
with the light of our love.

Reveal to us
  our hidden home
  that lies deeply buried
  in the secret heart
  of your midnight light.

STUDY THE COINCIDENCES IN YOUR LIFE.
THEY ARE GATEWAYS
THROUGH THE ILLUSION
OF LIFE BEING WHAT YOU THINK IT IS.

CHAPTER NINE

Losing Your Way

*T*he following poem describes what it's like to lose your way in life, and then find it again with the help of these six practices. It spells out the many ways we can get lost when we begin to lose our connection with the higher reality and, instead, begin to identify with our own egos. It is a reminder that when we become attached to a false idea of ourselves and regard ourselves as merely body, mind or emotions, material objects can become more important to us than what underlies them. The poem traces the process of refusing to maintain life's illusory reality to focus instead on that which lies deeper, the only source of true contentment and satisfaction.

LOST AND FOUND

Have you ever felt as if you'd lost your
*   way,*
*   as if you'd lost your self?*

Have you ever felt impossibly engulfed
*   in unending waves of unbearable*
*   emotion,*

so that you fly outward in a million
*   directions,*
*   inwardly knowing that none are quite*
*   right?*
*   Have you ever felt unendurably alone,*
*   your true uniqueness and beauty*
*   unseen by anyone—*
*   even yourself?*

Is your mind a galloping whirlwind of
unrest,
uncontrollably leaping from
why, to how, to maybe, to what if,
all the while fleeing from
the black face of hopelessness
and quiet desperation
which threatens to engulf you
if you tarry even an instant?

Inside you scream your hope and despair
as you wallow painfully off balance,
searching for the calm
in the storm of unknowing,
even as you sometimes almost
glimpse

that which you once knew,
as it continually dances just
outside of your grasping.

So you put on your brave face,
covering your anger with smiles,
searching for happiness
from behind veiled eyes
among the empty pleasures
of this world,
fooling everyone—
even yourself.

For a time you escape,
  two steps ahead of the persistent
    tormentor,
  that voice that in the still night
  tells you that all is not right,
  that your transient pleasure
  is built on shifting sand,
  and at any moment
  the change is to come.

You're not alone in these feelings.
Look around you,
  see the shape of the world
  in its game of desperate folly,
  all running madly,
  searching for more,
  racing blindly
  on a path of destruction.
There is a way out,
  my fellow life-traveler.
There's a path through this madness.
It's simple yet difficult.
You have only to dare
  to drop all falseness
  as you step through the mirror.

It begins by looking the demon in the eye,
  letting the emptiness catch up with
    you.
Stop all running,
  and dive deeply into the torment,

having no answers for awhile.
Relax and follow the true path,
        that, if you know how to listen,
        is entirely within you.

Be brave,
        and know that in this, too,
        you are not alone.
Stop condemning yourself.
Forgive,
        and endlessly accept.
Don't be afraid if you falter,
        for you will many times.

Join your fellow travelers.
Let their words and experiences
        remind you of the Way,
        again—and again.
Relax,
        and breathe deeply,
        trusting the comforter within,
        and begin the most exciting journey
        of your life.

Fearlessly tame your tyrannical mind,
        which mercilessly batters you with
        conjecture, imaginings, false logic,
        and engulfs you in its own limiting
                viewpoints
        of what's possible and not possible,
        of what's real and not real,
        and who you are or are not.

Forget your endless focus
        on yourself,
        and instead gaze into the limitless
                space
        between thoughts.
Dive completely
        into that great silence,
        and with perfect attention

let your mind rest
        in an ocean of calm.

Slowly and deeply
        draw the life-giving breath into your
                body.
Let go,
        and shed all fear, doubt and sadness.
Then slowly, oh so slowly,
        a faint whisper of peace
        will steal through
        the walls of your uncertainty.

And drop by precious drop
        will crumble the protections
        of your vulnerability,
        and with painful sweetness
        will be pierced
        your too well-protected heart.
Your silent screams of despair
        will turn to blossoms of peace.

Here will emerge your true strength,
   strength that is not rigid or blind,
   but flows as water and bends as a
      windblown tree.

And what will stand clearly revealed
   in silence that speaks,
   is You,
   fearlessly radiant,
   beyond all limitation and projection.

Then you will know the unknowable,
   and remember that which was lost.
You will walk unafraid and undisturbed
   through this world madness,
   and partake of the sweet essence
   within all that is seen and unseen.
You will know love,
   beyond all understanding—

And you will be happy.

Growth along this path of self-discovery is very rarely linear. Unlike having a regular teacher who's job it is to help prevent you from wandering too far from the path, when you only have your inner voice to guide you, you may not even realize how far you've wandered until life itself reminds you; it usually does this by becoming increasingly difficult, complex, or unhappy.

In general, it takes constant vigilance and honest self-evaluation to both stay on the path and return when you've wandered. However, there are a few traditional problems and "warning signs" that you can be aware of. These will help signal that you're "off track."

Mistaking Your Own Desires for the Inner Truth

It's not always easy to discriminate between the voice of truth and your own desires, between what you want to be true and what actually is. Over and over again you'll mistake the voice of your limited ego for reality, hearing its voice instead of the guidance of your inner soul.

Ultimately, all you can do is learn to recognize and trust the guiding Inner Spirit, and this learning process is what this journey is about (this is where prayer helps). Though you may be temporarily unable to hear the voice of the guiding Inner Spirit, it will never leave you. Do the best that you can do, trusting that if you're wrong, you'll be corrected (for you will be many times). Then surrender again. Learn to recognize the messages that life offers, asking your to pay attention or change, to focus more on the truth of the Inner Spirit. When you are feeling emotionally scattered or insecure, ask what Spirit is trying to teach you. When you are physically ill, look for the lesson. When you lose a job, or your business isn't going well, or when a relationship starts getting rocky, stop, quiet your mind, and seek the lessons that may be present in these challenges.

The Lesson

Years ago, as I was sitting with my Native American teacher, he told me that I was stubborn. Now, he teaches with few words, so when he says something like this I know that it is an important teaching for me. I was immediately puzzled, so I asked him, "Grandfather, I just follow what I hear inside me. How can I go against this, even if someone else tells me I must do something or believe something differently? Is this what you mean by stubborn? If so, I don't know what else I can follow!"

I expected him to tell me more about what he meant, or guide me in a direction, but he just looked at me without replying. So I started working with this issue. I didn't like the idea that I was stubborn. It meant to me that I was rigidly sticking to my own beliefs, insisting on my own way instead of hearing what was really true. The idea that I was doing this was awful to me! I wanted to root it out of me, so I decided to think of myself as stubborn and see if I could behave any differently.

However, as I tried to do this, I immediately had a problem. I didn't really know how to go against what I felt to be true deep down inside of me. Each time that I tried to not be stubborn, and follow someone else's direction that differed from my own inner guidance, it seemed as though I lost my own center. Again and again I kept confronting the same dilemma; how could I possibly go against myself? How could following what I heard to be true inside of me be called stubborn or egotistical?

I wrestled with this problem for about two years. Finally, when I was again working with my teacher, I brought up the subject of my stubbornness. "Grandfather," I asked, "I've tried not to be stubborn for the last two years. I've tried to experience myself as stubborn. However, I can't in any integrity go against what I feel inside of myself. Can you help me with this?" He started chuckling as he answered, "Granddaughter, you're not stubborn. I just wanted you to work with this so that you'd know for sure what stubbornness was and was not. I wanted you to investigate your own ego and know the difference between this and what was truly the voice of Spirit. Now you have learned."

I immediately understood the teaching. By this lesson I learned not only the difference between stubborness and following my own inner integrity, but I also learned the importance of continually remaining on the outlook for the intrusion of my egoistic desires masquerading as Truth. This was especially important if I was to do the healing and other work that I was learning from him. This would keep me from getting lost. I learned that I couldn't rest my vigilance, thinking that I was somehow above succumbing to my own ego. For this reason I must always be willing to listen to others, understanding their criticisms both as valid teachings for me and as mere projections of their own minds. Even as I study myself in the mirror of other's projections, however, ultimately I must still follow my own inner sense of integrity and Truth. Finally, I learned to accept that as much as the voice of the Spirit was within my own soul, I was also as fallible a human being as anyone else. What a wonderful lesson!

This is why you continually surrender yourself to the Higher Spirit. This is why you do everything you can to keep the lines of communication open between you and your inner Self. For as long as you keep renewing your intention to be aligned with that which is most real, you'll not be allowed to wander far.

Signs and Guidelines to Know That You're Lost

Here are a few guidelines to tell if you're "off track." First, you're lost if you find yourself thinking that you're more important, more special or better than other people. This doesn't mean that you shouldn't experience your own intrinsic value. Nor is it wrong to feel the special expansiveness within you or the power that comes from your alignment with Spirit. On the contrary, you need to allow yourself to experience everything about yourself. You're only misguided if you feel that you're in some way set apart from others. In thinking of yourself as special or different, you've lost the awareness of your essential oneness with every other human being and with all creation.

Another way to become lost is to start thinking that you know more than you do. As soon as you abandon the "Zen-mind" or "empty mind," thinking that you "know," you actually don't. In order to make the judgment "I know," you need to separate yourself from the moment to moment experience of what you're observing in order to define or explain it to yourself. When you do that, you don't really know anything.

The ultimate form of thinking that you "know," is to think of yourself as enlightened. *As soon as you think you're enlightened, know that you're not.* An enlightened person doesn't set herself apart in order to make that kind of definition. In fact, you're lost as soon as you define yourself in any way, because who you are is totally beyond definition or explanation.

These thoughts and feelings about yourself may be very subtle, not readily obvious to you or anyone else. You may not even verbalize these opinions, but only hold them as conscious or subconscious attitudes. These feelings or opinions with which you define yourself may be as mere pinpricks in your consciousness, barely signaling their existence and noticeable only if you're already looking for them. They may be disguised in altruistic or enlightened "wrappings," signaling their presence with a barely noticed sense of inner disquiet.

Look for signs of pride, of greed or covetousness. If you find yourself being defensive, or self-righteousness, even slightly, know that you're probably identifying with a false idea of yourself. If you find that you're lying, withholding or being dishonest in any way, know that you're not experiencing your true self. If your heart is closed, fearful or angry, you've temporarily lost your way. So, too, if you find that you're doing something that's not in alignment with your own sense of inner integrity.

Look for signs of self-righteousness. It's a common mistake to begin thinking that your path is the only way, or the best way. Instead, remember that your way is just that—your way. Just because it's the way that's working for you doesn't mean that it will work best for everyone else. If you find yourself putting yourself above another by criticizing them, remember my Native American Grandfather's saying:

> "Whenever you find yourself pointing your finger at someone, remember that you also have three fingers pointing back at you!"

Finally, if you lack a sense of inner fulfillment, or if you find that you're not deeply content, know that you've not yet awakened to your true reality.

Be suspect when you say or do things to excuse your own behavior. Chances are that you're doing something or acting in some way that is not of the highest integrity. Any time that you find yourself saying or acting as if the ends justify some questionable means, stop and meditate on your behavior. The means are just as important as the ends, sometimes more important. In other words, how you get something done is just as important as getting it done.

If you find yourself saying, for example, "Well, I know this looks bad, but something good is going to come of it," investigate your action thoroughly.

New Abilities

*A*fter doing the six practices in this book, you may be able to see the "larger picture" in life, seeing solutions to problems when others don't. You may experience some of the powers associated with the opening of the "third eye," abilities in your life that most people would consider "special" or "miraculous." You can use these powers to help others. However, that, too, can be a trap. As with any use of these powers, it's easy for you to start thinking or feeling yourself as somehow above or better than the person that you're helping. To avoid this tendency, if you elect to help others with any of these powers, constantly contemplate this:

WHO IS HELPING WHOM?
PERHAPS YOU'RE BEING HELPED MORE
BY BEING ABLE TO GIVE
THAN THE ONE WHO IS RECEIVING.

You can further avoid losing your way with respect to these powers if you bear in mind that you do not *have* these powers. Instead, they merely flow through you. Also, remember that these special abilities and powers only seem miraculous if you're identified only with physical reality. As you do the practices in the book and begin to experience a more limitless realm of reality, beyond just the physical, you'll find that these abilities are natural in the subtle realms where they exist. They are as natural as gravity is to the physical realm, and like gravity, have their own laws and behaviors. When you become aware of subtleties beyond the physical, you'll find that these powers lose their sense of specialness. To think of yourself as special because you experience them is as foolish as thinking of yourself as special because you experience the effects of gravity.

Many scriptures recommend that these powers not be sought after, or that you ignore them if they come to you so that they don't cause you to lose your way. If these powers come to you, whether you use them or not, to avoid losing your way, meditate on the Self that has the powers.

To Take Personal Credit
For having Spiritual Powers
Is To See Precious Pearls
Turn To Mudballs.

Confusion, Clinging and Running Away

When you find yourself lost in your day-to-day living, find your way back by doing the six practices given in this book. Do them even if you think they're not working, even if they're hard and even if you're still confused. Rather than always being a sign that you're off the path, your confusion may be a sign that you're moving to a new level of realization. When you're feeling lost, it's sometimes hard to tell. Rather than abandoning your practice at such times, do just the opposite. Be patient and keep on doing the practices anyway. If you do that, your confusion will clear and you'll likely discover a whole new level of meaning in your life.

Don't try to hang onto your happiness, grasping and hoarding it as a miser does his pennies, for then it will only disappear. When you try to hold onto happiness, you're only cutting it off from its source. Any time that you start grasping for happiness, trying to keep it from disappearing, you're succumbing to fear. You're stumbling back into the illusory belief that happiness is dependent on the events of your life instead of experiencing it as arising from within your own heart. If you mistakenly start believing that it's coming from what you do or have, no longer can you be open to life's constant changes because you'll be busy trying to prevent any "bad" changes from happening (which is *impossible*). When you succumb to the belief that your happiness depends on what happens to you, your heart can only close in fear and distrust. Then, happiness is impossible. Instead of trying to stop life from changing in the fear that you'll experience something that will make you unhappy, let go and let yourself experience the happiness that springs from within your own heart.

Next, don't run from your fears. It is fear that makes you afraid to face your deepest self and discover your true beauty. It's fear that hides you from wisdom, that drives you to illness and depletes your energy. The more you try to escape fear, the greater its power will become. As soon as you look it squarely in the face, however, its power starts to dwindle. Instead of running from your fears, be willing to experience them. Let them lose their mysterious and terrifying qualities as you begin to know them intimately. When you do that, you'll find that they aren't bigger or more powerful than you are. Only by facing your fears can you defeat them.

The same thing is true when you're feeling depression or anxiety. Instead of running from it, or letting it run away with you, the most important thing to do is to continually bring yourself back to the present. In the process of continually bringing yourself back to the here and now, observe the interlocking mechanisms of thought and feeling that cause you to focus on the past or future and thus become depressed or anxious. As you do this, not only will you find that your depression or anxiety is gradually disappearing, but you'll notice yourself becoming progressively calm and relaxed.

Roadmaps for Enlightened Living

Though it is true that your ultimate guide is your own inner sense of truth, there are some general "rules of action" that can also help guide you. These rules, followed by spiritually oriented people from antiquity to the present time, are not meant to constrain you. On the contrary, they exist as guidelines to help you find your way when you're confused, and to re-enter the path when you've lost your way or when you're about to lose your way. If you find that your actions conflict with these guidelines, take another look at what you're do-ing or about to do. It's likely that you're acting out of alignment with your deepest inner integrity.

The first guideline is this: "Love your neighbor as yourself." This not only tells you to love your neighbor, but also tells you to love yourself. Sometimes it's easier to show love and caring for someone else than it is for yourself. How often do you find yourself more forgiving of others than yourself, for example? How often do you find yourself excusing someone else's behavior while you end-lessly berate yourself for the same thing? When you love your neighbor as yourself, it means to forgive, to accept and to honor yourself as well as the other. It means to have empathy and to be concerned for the welfare of both yourself and others. For example, if you find that your actions violate anyone's honor or fail to accept anyone as a fellow human being, even yourself, they are leading you away from the path to realization. If you find that what you're doing helps you at the expense of another's well-being, it's similarly harm-ful. Remember, you can't buy your own freedom at the expense of others. You'll experience no real peace unless you're willing for its benefits to extend to all, not just yourself.

The next guide to enlightened action might seem equally as familiar. However, just because it's familiar doesn't mean that it isn't powerful. This helpful guideline is the ancient *Ten Commandments* given to Moses long ago. Rather than dismissing these as restrictive laws that aren't in tune with today's realities, you'll find that when you meditate on their deeper meanings they merely reflect what is alignment with integrity or deeper Truth. You'll find that any action that's in alignment with Truth is seldom, if ever, in violation of these. Instead of feeling restricted by these laws, then, understand them as suggestions for "right action," or for that action that helps you to stay on the path. If you find that your actions seem to violate one or more of these commandments, be wary. Investigate further to see if they're in alignment with you own inner honesty and integrity.

The next set of guidelines, called the *Five Basic Precepts*, stem from the Buddhist tradition. Though they may not be as familiar as the *Ten Commandments*, they are equally as powerful. To follow them creates protection, helping you refrain from actions that produce pain and suffering as a result of greed, hatred or delusion. Following them helps you to act in a way that produces lightness and clarity of mind instead of mental darkness. They will help free your mind from remorse and anxiety based on guilt about what you're doing or what you've done in the past. When you're freed from guilt, you can more easily bring your mind into the present so that you can experience the true reality. Following these precepts, then, can provide a basis for your further spiritual development. *The Five Precepts* are as follows:

The Five Precepts

1. "REFRAIN FROM KILLING." When you follow this precept, you honor the desire of all beings to be free from pain, to live and to be happy. It will allow you to develop a reverence for all forms of life, which will lead to a much lighter state of mind.

2. "REFRAIN FROM STEALING." This means to refrain from taking what doesn't belong to you. If you desire to take what isn't yours, you're succumbing to the illusion that the things you have will bring you happiness.

3. "REFRAIN FROM SEXUAL MISCONDUCT." This is another way that the concept of "adultery" can be understood. You can understand this precept as meaning to refrain from all sensual actions that can cause pain, disturbance or harm to others—and thus to yourself.

4. "REFRAIN FROM WRONG SPEECH." This not only means to refrain from lying, but to cultivate speech that creates harmony, gentleness and unity between others and in the environment around you. How often speech is wasted in useless or harmful gossip, or harsh or abusive language. How often words are used

carelessly, without thought to their often far-reaching effects. Such harshness in speech creates harshness within you, within others, and within your environment, whether it is intended or not. Be aware of your words, for if spoken with care and gentleness, they have the power to create peace within your mind.

5. "REFRAIN FROM TAKING INTOXICANTS WHICH CLOUD YOUR MIND AND MAKE IT DULL." When you're walking this path of mental clarity, it's not helpful to use substances which lead your mind back to the darkness of illusion, or impede its ability to concentrate or observe. This doesn't necessarily mean that you should never have a drink of wine or other alcoholic substance, only that you should avoid using drink as a means of avoidance. Also, there are some ancient spiritual traditions which use mind-altering substances to teach or guide, and to open the mind (temporarily), to deeper realities of which it is usually unaware. Be aware of using mind-altering substances, especially without a guide or teacher. It is a common mistake to think that your mind is being expanded when it's actually being dulled or mislead with the extra sensations that you're experiencing. Also, it's often the case that you begin to feel as if you can't experience the clarity of heightened awareness without the use of the drugs. Rather then leading to enlightenment then, this dependency instead leads to your "endarkenment."

Finally, there are many highly developed teachers from times past that have left behind simple guidelines for behavior which will help you stay on the path of discovery. One of these was left by my teacher, Neem Karoli Baba. His very simple instruction is this: "Love, Serve, and Remember." Yet another instruction, left by the great teacher Meher Baba, is "Be Happy." These guidelines are seemingly simplistic. Yet, as you continue to contemplate them and use them in your daily life, you'll see that they offer a complete guide for acting in a way that leads to realization of the one Higher Spirit that lies as the essence of your own being.

As effective as these guidelines are for helping you stay on the path in the everyday world, don't use them to ignore the wisdom of Truth's voice which speaks inside your own heart. Rather than replacing this inner voice, let these guidelines help lead you past the deafening desires of your limited ego so that you can instead hear the clear voice of Truth that lies revealed within your own soul.

ARISE

Stand with head held high
    among the shambles of your life,
    knowing that you're not judged
    by the things that you do or don't
       have,
    or by what you've done or not done.

But only by the quality of your life,
    and by your heart,
    by that which you've given,
    even if just a kind word
    to one who is in need.

Dwell not harshly on yourself, my friend.
Resist drowning yourself in sadness,
    embarrassment, anger, or other false
      dreams.
Think no more of what might be
    or what could have been.

What is,
    is now.
And you are about to rise phoenix-like
    from the ashes of your ruins,
    onward to life's next adventure,
    each pain a learning,
    and each closing door an opening.

Recognize yourself,
*   to be a child of the Spirit,*
*   just as you are—completely.*
Hold your head high in this knowing,
*   and rest in its comfort.*

Look with equal eye
*   on your successes and failures.*
Sift through the pain and the pleasure,
*   gleaning what's to be learned,*

Oh friend, move on to the next play
*   in life's endless game,*
*   knowing that your true winning*
*   is not in having, getting or doing,*
*   but only in the truth of your own*
*   being.*

So know that it's never the end,
*   but always the beginning,*
*   each new breath an opportunity,*
*   a declaration of freedom,*
*   and of life born anew.*

To Be Enlightened
Is To
Lighten Up.

Homecoming

As you do the six practices you become increasingly aware of an ancient spiritual truth: To be born is incredibly precious, for it is only in our birth that we have a chance to become awakened to our true nature. Of this entire worldly creation, only humans have the particular ability to be conscious of themselves as separate entities apart from the creation surrounding them. Only humans have the opportunity to discover their own divinity. Does a flower think of itself? Does an animal question itself? Does a fish ponder the water in which it swims, or a bird think about the air in which it flies? Everything in this physical world exists together in harmony,

according to its own nature and in accordance
with natural laws. No other being on this planet,
other than a human being, desires to be anything
other than what it is.

No other being on this planet is as separated from itself as we human beings. This is both our curse and our blessing. Look at the effects caused by such separation, both within ourselves and in our environment. This disharmony, this sense of separation causes untold suffering. Yet, this same suffering also causes us to search for its cause and seek its ending. In seeking its end, we find our awakening. This is the hidden blessing contained in the separation brought about by birth. This is the priceless jewel that is contained in the heart of our pain and our suffering.

To be born is to journey into darkness, into an illusory separation from the oneness in which you have your being. It is to be set apart from yourself in order to discover yourself. Being born is like acquiring a mirror in which you have an opportunity to see yourself because you now have a separate image that is apart from you (your body, mind, etc.). However, when you contemplate this image of yourself in the mirror, you eventually see that in essence you're not really separate from it. The separation that you experience is merely an illusion. If you take the mirror away, you're forced to experience yourself differently, finding that you still exist only if you shift your attention inward to your own essence. (If you don't shift your attention inward when the mirror is removed, you no longer experience yourself.)

Life is like this. It's not until you shift your gaze away from the mirror, from the appearance of yourself, that you can be awakened to your inner essence or your true nature. Only then can you know the reality of oneness that is contained in the illusion of separateness. However, in order to first see yourself, it's necessary to be born, because without birth you have no mirror.

Dying is like removing the mirror from in front of you and losing the view of your face. Ultimately, just as your image leaves when you put down the mirror, when you breathe your last breath, and leave your body with its ever-changing thoughts and emotions, this world vanishes as a dream, leaving nothing but the reality of Truth and love, of the reality beyond form, space or time. All images and all separateness disappears. All that you have left when you die is the essential reality of your true Self.

If you haven't experienced your existence apart from the picture in the mirror, you won't be able to experience yourself when the mirror is removed. If you're asleep to your Self now, you'll be asleep to your Self when you die. Likewise, if you know yourself apart from the image in the mirror, you will continue to exist with the mirror's removal. If you're awake to your Self now, so will you be after death. If you are so awakened, there will be no death at all, only a continuing Self-awareness.

Don't waste this precious opportunity of awakening to your own potential that your birth brings to you. Who knows if or when you'll have another chance? As the great Sufi mystic Kabir says:

"Friend, hope for the Guest while you are alive.
Jump into experience while you are alive!
Think—and think—while you are alive.
What you call "salvation" belongs
to the time before death.
If you don't break your ropes while you're alive,
do you think ghosts will do it after?"

— TRANSLATION BY ROBERT BLY

Do these six practices to awaken and discover your Self. Search for your own essential, unending reality that is still present when the "mirror" of body, mind, emotion and all other appearances is removed. You don't need to retreat from the world to do this. Nor do you need to distinguish between the spiritual and earthly life. Let the everyday world be your workshop, for all your tools are right here before you. Observe, be present-centered, remember, surrender and meditate, all the time following the guidance of the Truth deep within your soul. Don't compromise. Be a warrior of Truth, refusing to sacrifice your own integrity upon the altar of convenience. Refuse to bow to the seductions of life's temporary illusions. Ask from the depths of your heart to be shown the Way, and you will surely be answered. Listen carefully to that answering voice of guidance within and learn to discriminate delusion from reality. Then you will know ignorance from wisdom.

May you be who you are, the infinite Self that exists beyond all rational understanding and the boundaries of individual ego, and know yourself as undying, unborn, timeless and formless, one with everything in the universe. May you surrender all doubt, anger and shame, letting your heart open to the depths of love, fearing no one and nothing, not even your own death. Surrender to the Beloved, who patiently lies waiting for you within the heart of your soul and be one with the endless Truth that forms the core of your being. For only then will you awaken to the joyful happiness of your own infinite aliveness and the unending peace of your soul's perfect freedom.

HOMECOMING

Sound the thousand winged trumpets!
Unfurl the golden flags of welcome!
Oh wandering one, you have at last
returned to the home of your birth.

With your shining countenance
and glorious star-lit eyes,
you return victorious,
cloaked in endless dreams made real.

Oh Pilgrim of the Spirit,
what star-filled lands
have you beheld with the knowing eyes
of your sky-clad soul!

How joyfully freedom's song
sings it's sweet abandonment
within the open chamber
of your sun-filled heart!

Free—free at last are thee!
Having sundered illusion's web of lies,
you now walk the clear skies
of what, before, you dared to dream!

Uma Silbey is president of *Uma Natural Gemstone Jewelry*, has authored two other books, and is an accomplished recording artist. She lives in West Marin County, California, where she enjoys a full family life with Steve, her husband, and two sons, Ram Paul and Luke.

OTHER BOOKS BY
UMA SILBEY

The Complete Crystal Guidebook
(A Bantam New Age Book)

Paul and Mary and their Magic Crystals
(a children's book available from Airo Press)

MUSIC BY UMA SILBEY
Cassettes and compact discs available through

AIRO AUDIO

Watergarden
Voyager
Healing
Relax
Crystals, Chakras, Color and Sound
Crystal Path
Vision Quest (by Bearheart)
Medicine Songs (by Bearheart)

Airo Press / Airo Audio
655-E Dubois St., San Rafael, California 94901 (415)453-8845